Everyman's Poetry

*Everyman, I will go with thee,
and be thy guide*

Algernon Charles Swinburne

Selected and edited by CATHERINE MAXWELL

Queen Mary and Westfield College, University of London

D1465124

EVERYMAN

J. M. Dent · London

This edition first published by Everyman Paperbacks in 1997
Selection, Introduction and other critical apparatus
© J. M. Dent 1997

J. M. Dent
Orion Publishing Group
Orion House
5 Upper St Martin's Lane,
London WC2H 9EA

Typeset by Deltatype Ltd, Birkenhead, Merseyside
Printed in Great Britain by
The Guernsey Press Co. Ltd, Guernsey, C.I.

British Library Cataloguing-in-Publication Data is available
upon request.

ISBN 0 460 87871 9

Contents

Note on the Author and Editor   v
Chronology of Swinburne's Life and Times   vi
Introduction   xii
Note on the Text   xviii

The Nightingale   3

From Poems and Ballads I (1866)
A Ballad of Life   4
A Ballad of Death   6
The Triumph of Time   10
Les Noyades   21
Itylus   23
Anactoria   25
Hermaphroditus   33
Fragoletta   35
Anima Anceps   37
In the Orchard   39
The Leper   40
Rondel   45
Before the Mirror   46
The Garden of Proserpine   48
The Sundew   51
Sapphics   52
August   55

From Songs Before Sunrise (1871)
Hertha   57
Genesis   64
Cor Cordium   66

From Poems and Ballads II (1878)
A Forsaken Garden   67
Relics   69
A Ballad of Dreamland   72
A Vision of Spring in Winter   73

From Songs of the Springtides (1880)
On the Cliffs   75

From Tristram of Lyonesse (1882)
from The Queen's Pleasance   87

From A Century of Roundels (1883)
The Lute and the Lyre   89
Plus Intra   89
The Roundel   90
Three Faces   90
On an Old Roundel   92
A Flower-Piece by Fantin   93

From A Midsummer Holiday and Other Poems (1884)
A Sea-Mark   93

From Poems and Ballads III (1889)
To a Seamew   94

From A Channel Passage and Other Poems (1904)
The Lake of Gaube   98
In a Rosary   100

Notes   102
Acknowledgements   110

Note on the Author and Editor

ALGERNON CHARLES SWINBURNE (1837–1909) is arguably the most important Victorian poet after Tennyson and Browning. The eldest child of Captain (later Admiral) Charles Henry and Lady Jane Swinburne, he grew up near East Dene on the Isle of Wight where the natural beauty of the shoreline made a lasting impression on him. He wrote his first verse during his schooling at Eton. In 1857, while at Balliol College, Oxford, he met the Pre-Raphaelites at work on the Oxford Union and began an important friendship with Dante Gabriel Rossetti. After university, he lived in London and started an active writing career. His first collection *Poems and Ballads* (1866) caused a sensation on account of the 'impropriety' of its subject matter. His later productions, which included drama, epic and political verse, roused less of a stir, but showed an impressive and successful experimentation with different poetic forms and subjects: he was an unrivalled metricist. In 1879, after a period of loneliness and alcoholism, Swinburne took out joint tenancy of No. 2 The Pines, Putney with his friend the novelist and critic Theodore Watts-Dunton. Watts-Dunton's tactful guardianship ensured that the last period of the poet's life proved happy and productive. Swinburne was a considerable critic as well as poet, and his literary and aesthetic essays proved influential for later writers such as Pater, Wilde and Yeats. His two novels *Lesbia Brandon* and *Love's Cross-Currents* and his letters have a wit and piquancy unique to English Victorian prose.

CATHERINE MAXWELL was educated at St Hugh's College, Oxford where she was British Academy Postdoctoral Fellow 1990–93. She is now Lecturer in English at Queen Mary and Westfield College, London University where she teaches specialist courses on Victorian poetry and prose. She has published articles on Browning, Swinburne and the Rossettis and is writing a book on Victorian male poets.

Chronology of Swinburne's Life

Year	Age	Life
1836		Marriage of Captain Charles Henry Swinburne and Lady Jane Hamilton
1837		(5 April) Birth of Algernon Charles Swinburne at 7 Chester Street, Grosvenor Place, London, the eldest of six children
1848	11	Swinburne prepared for Eton by Rev. Foster Fenwick, Vicar of Brook, Isle of Wight
1849	12	Arrives at Eton. Writes tragedy *The Unhappy Revenge*. Visits Wordsworth with parents
1852	15	Wins Prince Consort's Prize for Modern Languages
1853	16	Leaves Eton. Sent to Cambo, Northumberland to be prepared for Oxford by Rev. John Wilkinson
1855	18	Tutored by Rev. Russell Woodford, Kempsford, Glos. Visits Germany with uncle
1856	19	(23 Jan.) Enters Balliol College, Oxford. Becomes member of the Old Mortality Society, an intellectual group founded by John Nichol
1857	20	Essays and poems in *Undergraduate Papers*, journal of Old Mortality. Fails to win the Newdigate poetry prize. Meets Morris, Jones and D. G. Rossetti at work decorating the Oxford Union
1858	21	(Jan.) Visits Tennyson at Farringford. Gains a second in Oxford Moderations examination; wins the Taylorian Scholarship in June
1859	22	Fails Classics examination and sent to read modern history with Rev. William Stubbs in Essex
1860	23	(May) Returns to Oxford and passes Classics examination, but leaves after withdrawing from his finals. Moves to London and publishes verse-plays *Rosamond* and *The Queen Mother*

Chronology of his Times

Year	Artistic Events	Historical Events
1832	Tennyson, *Poems*	First Reform Act
1837	Carlyle, *French Revolution*	Accession of Queen Victoria
1842	Tennyson, *Poems*	Chartist Riots
1845	Browning, *Dramatic Romances and Lyrics*	Famine in Ireland (45–51)
1848	Formation of the Pre-Raphaelite Brotherhood	Democratic revolutions in France, Germany, Austria, Poland and parts of Italy
1849	Arnold, *The Strayed Reveller*	
1850	Wordsworth, *The Prelude*	Death of Wordsworth
1855	Tennyson, *Maud, and Other Poems*	
1856	Morris and Burne-Jones, *The Oxford & Cambridge Magazine* Barrett Browning, *Aurora Leigh*	
1857	Baudelaire, *Les Fleurs du Mal*	Indian Mutiny
1858	Morris, *The Defence of Guenevere*	Orsini fails to assassinate Napoleon III
1859	Tennyson, *Idylls of the King*	Pope refuses to renounce temporal power
1860	Collins, *The Woman in White*	

Year	Age	Life
1861	24	Visits Mentone and Italy. Given £400 p.a. by his father to pursue a literary career in London.
1862	25	Poetry and essays in *The Spectator*, including review of Baudelaire's *Les Fleurs du Mal*
1863	26	Takes up residence with Rossetti at Tudor House, Cheyne Walk, Chelsea. Develops close friendship with the painter Simeon Solomon. Death of favourite sister, Edith. Begins *Atalanta in Calydon*
1864	27	Travels in Italy and meets Landor. Leaves Tudor House.
1865	28	(March) *Atalanta in Calydon*. Family move to 'Holmwood', Oxfordshire. (June.) Marriage of Mary Gordon. (Nov.) *Chastelard: A Tragedy*
1866	29	*Poems and Ballads* published by Moxon's, withdrawn, and then republished by John Camden Hotten. *Notes on Poems and Reviews* to address the critical furore
1867	30	Meets Mazzini and is encouraged to write poems for the cause of Italian liberty. Has brief affair with the circus-rider Adah Menken
1868	31	*William Blake: A Critical Essay*
1871	34	*Songs before Sunrise*. Severe illness resulting from alcoholism. His father removes him to Holmwood to recuperate
1872	35	Returns to London and replies to Robert Buchanan's attack on himself and Rossetti ('The Fleshly School of Poetry') in *Under the Microscope*.
1874	37	*Bothwell: A Tragedy*
1875	38	*George Chapman: A Critical Essay*, *Songs of Two Nations*, *Essays and Studies*
1876	39	Second classical verse drama *Erectheus: A Tragedy*
1877	40	*A Note on Charlotte Brontë*. Death of Admiral Swinburne. *A Year's Letters* (later known as *Love's Cross-Currents*) appears in serial form
1878	41	*Poems and Ballads: Second Series*

Year	Artistic Events	Historical Events
1861	D. G. Rossetti, *The Early Italian Poets* Death of Elizabeth Barrett Browning	Death of Prince Albert; American Civil War begins
1862	Christina Rossetti, *Goblin Market* Death of Elizabeth Siddal	
1864	Browning, *Dramatis Personae*	Kingsley-Newman controversy; Death of Landor
1865	Arnold, *Essays in Criticism*	American Civil War ends
1866	Christina Rossetti, *The Prince's Progress*	
1867	Arnold, *New Poems* Death of Baudelaire	Second Reform Act
1868	Browning, *The Ring and the Book*	Gladstone succeeds Disraeli as prime minister
1870	D. G. Rossetti, *Poems*	Franco-Prussian War (70–72); Elementary Education Act
1871	Christina Rossetti, *SingSong*	Paris Commune; King Victor Emmanuel ruler of a fully united Italy
1872	George Eliot, *Middlemarch* Tennyson, *Poems*	
1874	Hardy, *Far From the Madding Crowd*	Disraeli prime minister
1875	Christina Rossetti, *Poems*	
1876	George Eliot, *Daniel Deronda*	Victoria proclaimed Empress of India
1878	Hardy, *The Return of the Native*	Whistler versus Ruskin

Year	Age	Life
1879	42	Swinburne now severely ill from alcoholism. (Sept.) Moves into No. 2 The Pines, Putney with Theodore Watts (Watts-Dunton after 1896) where he spends the rest of his life
1880	43	*Songs of the Springtides, Studies in Song, The Heptalogia*
1881	44	*Mary Stuart: A Tragedy*
1882	45	*Tristram of Lyonesse and Other Poems.* Visits Hugo in Paris accompanied by Watts
1883	46	*A Century of Roundels*
1884	47	*A Midsummer Holiday and Other Poems*
1885	48	*Marino Faliero* (drama)
1886	49	*Miscellanies* and *A Study of Victor Hugo*
1887	50	*Locrine: A Tragedy*
1888	51	Attacks Whistler in an article 'Mr Whistler's Lecture on Art'
1889	52	*Poems and Ballads: Third Series*
1892	55	*The Sisters: A Tragedy* (contemporary drama). Death of General Disney Leith
1893	56	Mary Disney Leith visits and corresponds
1894	57	*Astrophel and Other Poems, Studies in Prose and Poetry*
1896	59	*The Tale of Balen.* Death of mother
1899	62	*Rosamund, Queen of the Lombards*
1903	63	Suffers first attack of pneumonia
1904	67	*A Channel Passage and Other Poems*
1905	68	*Love's Cross-Currents.* Watts-Dunton marries his secretary Clara Reich
1907	70	Refuses honorary degree from Oxford
1908	71	*The Age of Shakespeare, The Duke of Gandia*
1909	72	(10 April) Dies from pneumonia at The Pines (15 April) Buried at Bonchurch, Isle of Wight

Year	Artistic Events	Historical Events
1880	Deaths of Eliot and Flaubert	Gladstone prime minister
1881	D. G. Rossetti, *Ballads and Sonnets*	Death of Disraeli; Married Woman's Property Act
1882	Christina Rossetti, *Poems, New Series* Death of D. G. Rossetti	
1883	Meredith, *Poems and Lyrics*	Fabian Society founded
1884	Browning, *Ferishtah's Fancies*	Third Reform Act
1885	Tennyson, *Tiresias and Other Poems*	Salisbury prime minister
1886	Kipling, *Departmental Ditties*	Gladstone's defeat on Home Rule for Ireland
1888	Death of Arnold	
1889	Death of Browning	
1892	Symons, *Silhouettes* Death of Tennyson	Gladstone prime minister
1894	Deaths of Christina Rossetti and Pater	Rosebery prime minister
1895	Hardy, *Jude the Obscure*	Trials of Wilde
1896	Death of Morris	
1899	Symons, *The Symbolist Movement in Literature*	Boer War (1899–1902)
1901		Death of Queen Victoria; Accession of Edward VII
1905		Campbell-Bannerman prime minister
1907	Kipling awarded Nobel Prize	
1908		Asquith prime minister
1908	Death of Meredith	
1910		Death of Edward VII

Introduction

In spite of a steadily growing interest in Swinburne's poetry among literary scholars and critics, his work is not well known by general readers. Yet many of his concerns – his search for meaning outside of orthodox religion, his candid treatment of erotic love and the vagaries of sexual identity, his refusal to divorce spirituality from sensuous matter and sensuality – are certain to appeal to a modern audience.

Censured during his lifetime for the scandalous nature of his subject matter, Swinburne was also highly regarded for his lyrical powers and technical brilliance. In 1869 the critic Alfred Austin berated Browning's verse as 'studious prose', Tennyson's as 'feminine' and Swinburne's as both 'feminine' and 'improper'. That Austin grudgingly saw Swinburne as the third party in this unholy 'Trinity of Song' is, nonetheless, proof of the poet's prominence at this time.[1] When Tennyson died in 1892, Queen Victoria remarked to Gladstone, 'I am told that Mr Swinburne is the best poet in my dominions.'[2] She voiced the prevailing critical opinion that Swinburne should be offered the laureateship, although Gladstone was to demur on the grounds that Swinburne's vociferous political views made him ineligible. In 1895, George Saintsbury, the great authority on English prosody, declared: 'I do not think that Mr Swinburne has ever written a single piece of verse that can be called bad, or that does not possess qualities of poetry which before his day would have sufficed to give any man high poetical rank.' Unsurpassed in his knowledge of French Aesthetic writing, Swinburne was a key figure in the emergence and development of Aesthetic and Decadent literature in England, and the influence of both his poetry and critical prose on Walter Pater, Oscar Wilde, Arthur Symons and W. B. Yeats is unquestionable.

With the onset of literary modernism Swinburne's standing declined, although recent research has shown that the female modernists, such as the American poet H. D., proved alive to the poet's exploration of the fluidities of gender and his acknowledgement of female creative power.[3] These writers valued him as a precursor and learned much from the complementary flexible rhythms, musicality of expression and metrical energy with which he invested these themes. While Ezra Pound was also of the opinion that 'No one else has made such music in English',[4] most of the male modernists were keen to dismiss Swinburne's verse as an object of juvenile enthusiasms. Though Swinburne's poetic influence can be detected in T. S. Eliot's poems, Eliot's unfortunately influential essay 'Swinburne as Poet' (1920), damned with faint praise and engendered a still prevalent view of Swinburne's poetic language as 'independent', only 'hallucinating' meaning, and lacking any genuine referential purpose.[5] Since Eliot, a succession of critics have either celebrated or deplored Swinburne's supposed linguistic self-referentiality without considering adequately whether reference to ideas, emotions, vision, the material world, might simply function differently in his work, occurring through suggestion, association, and the affective emphases of rhythm.

The acceptance of unexamined critical commonplaces, coupled with a very thin knowledge of the poet's work and interests, dogs Swinburne criticism. It is still possible for a major critic of Victorian poetry to declare that 'arguably he produced nothing new'[6] after *Atalanta in Calydon* (Swinburne's poetic drama of 1865), while providing no evidence of having read any of the poetry after *Poems and Ballads* (1866). Readers of Swinburne's later poetry can easily refute the claim of non-development. His Arthurian epic *Tristram of Lyonesse* (1882), now considered by many to be his masterpiece, is his mature expression of an alternative spirituality, of 'the impulses to unity, transcendence, to an ecstatic experience of the one life immanent in linear and cyclical time'.[7] In the extract chosen for this selection (p. 87), the passionate love-making of Tristram and Iseult in the woods near Tintagel, an experience in which 'Sense into sense and spirit in spirit melt' (1. 380), becomes the expression of the symphonic energies of nature. This sense of the complex and mysterious interconnectedness of things undergoes further exploration in the late fine nature poems represented here by the magnificent 'Lake of Gaube' (p. 98).

While *Poems and Ballads I* will always remain central to any reading of Swinburne on account of its literary innovation and its unique historical impact, the later collections such as *Songs of the Springtides*, *Studies in Song*, *Astrophel* and *A Channel Passage* contain a quantity of considerable poems. Like many voluminous oeuvres,

Swinburne's has its fair share of repetition and verse which is workmanlike rather than absorbing, and readers sometimes have to dig deep, but there is more than enough strong poetry to refute the often-heard claim that he wrote nothing of value in his Putney years. The length of these poems and the introductory nature of this edition prevent the inclusion of 'Thalassius', 'Elegy' (for the explorer Richard Burton), 'By the North-Sea', 'A Nympholept', 'Loch Torridon', and others, but it is hoped that the selection will encourage interested readers to discover these for themselves. Also omitted for reasons of length is Swinburne's more obviously political verse from *Songs Before Sunrise*. However, I include the centrepiece of this collection, 'Hertha', which is not only Swinburne's hymn to the creative principle and life-force (envisaged as female power) but a statement of belief in humankind's ability to come of age, to outgrow restricting creeds and bring about conditions of universal freedom. Accompanying 'Hertha' is the sonnet 'Cor Cordium' in praise of Shelley, whom Swinburne admired for his dual commitment to poetry and libertarian politics.

This Everyman edition inevitably takes its largest group of poems from *Poems and Ballads I*, although some of the longer, more famous poems such as 'Dolores' and 'Laus Veneris' have been omitted in order to include other less well known but equally interesting pieces such as 'August', 'Hermaphroditus' and 'Itylus'. 'The Triumph of Time' has been included, as it seems that no selection is complete without it. Its imagery – the sea as a transcendent power and mother of all things, immersion as mergence, as birth, death, dream consciousness and sexual consummation – pulsates throughout Swinburne's work. Its themes of unreciprocated or lost love, the abandoned male lover (an unusual subject as Classical and Romantic traditions prefer to concentrate on the deserted woman), memory, desire and temporal transmutation, are ones to which Swinburne will return again and again. The other poems taken from *Poems and Ballads* enlarge these themes.

As various critics have noted, Swinburne is fascinated by opposites and the places where they meet and merge. In his appreciation of 'the divine contraries of life' ('Genesis', p. 64), he proves himself heir to William Blake whose work he admired and promoted and to Charles Baudelaire. Baudelaire's *Les Fleurs du Mal* (1857) finds its closest English equivalent in *Poems and Ballads I*. For Swinburne the merging contraries of life and death, natural and unnatural, tragedy and triumph, beauty and ugliness, good and evil, pleasure and pain, love and hate, body and spirit, male and female are of fundamental importance and nowhere is their fusion better evidenced than in his examination of gender and sexuality. Central to Swinburne's poetic vision is the mergence of male and female, whether figured as an act of heterosexual intercourse, as the hermaphrodite, androgyne or dual-sexed being, or as the figure of the lesbian or homosexual man (who in nineteenth-century gender typology was thought to be a manly woman or womanly man). Sexual union as spiritual consummation is the longed-for but often elusive desire of many poems, while in others 'ambiguously' sexed and gendered beings symbolise either the power of art and imagination to make artificial creations of beauty out of many divergent forces or, alternatively, the figure of the poet or artist. As Swinburne was to assert, 'great poets are bisexual; male and female at once'.[8]

This also explains Swinburne's passionate sense of kinship with Sappho, the classical Greek woman poet, whom he considered 'as beyond all question the greatest poet that ever lived'.[9] In poems like 'Anactoria' and 'Sapphics', Sappho's lesbianism is openly celebrated for the first time in English poetry since Donne's 'Sappho to Philaenis', and her verse is seen as transcendent. In 'Anactoria', Sappho speaks of how in death she and her song will become part of the music of the constantly changing natural world: 'I Sappho shall be one with all these things,/With all high things for ever' (p. 32) – a vision which anticipates the world-song of *Tristram of Lyonesse*. In voicing Sappho – and he brilliantly weaves her poetic fragments into his verse – Swinburne blurs boundaries by becoming one with her, absorbing her and her strength into the substance of his own poetry. While his treatment of lesbian sexuality in 'Anactoria' may not please some modern tastes, Swinburne discovers in Sappho the Romantic type of the alienated artist who forgoes the regular rewards of everyday life, but experiences its deepest pains and pleasures, expressing them with supreme eloquence. The great artist may be 'sterile' with regard to such human concerns as marriage and reproduction, but is compensated through the immortalising power of creation. Sappho's apocryphal suicidal leap into the sea is seen by Swinburne not as tragedy, but as energy triumphantly returning to its source. Her mergence with the 'great mother' gives Swinburne one more reason to love the sea and flood his verse with its rhythms and energies.

If the sea is the primary place of mergence and fusion, gardens and orchards are hardly less important for meetings and unions, for scenes of failed or achieved love. Certain of these poems including 'A Ballad of Life', 'A Forsaken Garden' and 'In a Rosary' follow the medieval tradition of the *hortus conclusus* where the garden is the site for visionary experience. The suspensive mood of these poems, the fact that they often occupy a twilit place in consciousness, is matched by Swinburne's use of synaesthesia or mixing of sense impressions, so that language, too, occupies a border-territory, describing multiple perceptions synchronously.

Consonant with his desire to marry opposites is Swinburne's fondness for the figure of the nightingale, a traditional poetic image for lyric song. The classical myth of the nightingale in which Philomela's pain and muteness is compensated by the gift of outstanding song enables a notion of lyric as uniting contrary emotions. While the nightingale poems of Coleridge, Keats and Arnold reach different conclusions about whether the bird's song is sad or happy, Swinburne embraces the complexity of mixed emotion. In 'Itylus', Philomela the nightingale mourns the murder of her nephew Itylus, while her sister, the swallow, chatters away in forgetful happiness. Yet throughout the exquisite cadences of Philomela's lament runs a subtle lilting counterpoint of joy as the reproachful nightingale mimes her sister's springtime happiness. This doubling of emotion is also increased by Philomela's evident melancholy pleasure in her own feats of memory and song. 'Anima Anceps', the 'sister' poem to 'Itylus', tells us to 'live like the swallow', but again its meditation on sorrow means that it inevitably mixes its emotional charge even while abjuring grief. Swinburne later informed his friend Theodore Watts-Dunton that he had abandoned the traditional story of Philomela for his own identification of the nightingale with Sappho, a change apparent in his wonderful late tribute to Sappho 'On the Cliffs'. However, traces of both identities are present in the fragment 'The Nightingale' with which this selection opens. This assured early lyric, probably written when the poet was at Oxford, provides an analogy between the mixed joy and sorrow of Philomela and Sappho's 'fierce sweetness'.

Swinburne wrote in praise of Blake that 'Even upon earth his vision was "twofold always": singleness of vision he scorned and feared'.[10] This selection introduces readers to Swinburne's own 'twofold vision' which, at its strongest, can recognise 'the power beyond all godhead which puts on / All forms of multitudinous unison'.[11] It is hoped that this glimpse will convince readers that Swinburne, whom Saintsbury called 'this most captivating of the poets of the second half of the nineteenth century in England', is also a poet for our time.

CATHERINE MAXWELL

References

1. Alfred Austin and George Saintsbury are cited from *Swinburne: The Critical Heritage*, ed. Clyde K. Hyder (London: Routledge & Kegan Paul, 1970), pp. 94, 105, 200, 199.

2. See Edmund Gosse, *The Life of Algernon Charles Swinburne* (London: Macmillan and Co., 1917), p. 277.

3. See Cassandra Laity, 'H. D. and A. C. Swinburne: Decadence and Sapphic Modernism', in *Lesbian Texts and Contexts: Radical Revisions*, eds Karla Jay and Joanne Glasgow (London: Onlywomen Press, 1992), pp. 217–40.

4. 'Swinburne versus his Biographers', in *Literary Essays of Ezra Pound*, ed. T. S. Eliot (London: Faber & Faber, 1954), p. 293.

5. See T. S. Eliot, *Selected Essays* (London: Faber & Faber, 1932), pp. 323–7.

6. Isobel Armstrong, *Victorian Poetry: Poetry, Poetics and Politics* (London and New York: Routledge, 1993), p. 417.

7. Rikky Rooksby, *The Whole Music of Passion: New Essays on Swinburne*, eds Rikky Rooksby and Nicholas Shrimpton (Aldershot and Vermont: Scolar Press, 1993), p. 86.

8. 'Tennyson and Musset', *Miscellanies* (London: Chatto & Windus, 1886), p. 221.

9. 'Sappho', *The Saturday Review* 117 (1914), 228.

10. *William Blake: A Critical Essay* (London: John Camden Hotten, 1868), p. 41.

11. *Tristram of Lyonesse* 9, 11. 4–5.

Note on the Text

With the exception of 'The Nightingale', which is reprinted from Georges Lafourcade, *Swinburne's Hyperion and Other Poems with an essay on Swinburne and Keats* (London: Faber and Gwyer, 1927), all poems are taken from *The Poems of Algernon Charles Swinburne*, 6 vols (London: Chatto & Windus, 1904), which is the most reliable collected edition available.

Algernon Charles Swinburne

The Nightingale

Thro' the thick throbbings of her trembling throat,
   Half stifled with its music, struggling gush'd
The torrent-tide of song, then free burst out
   And in a tempest whirl of melody rush'd
Thro' the stirred boughs. The young leaves on the trees
Flutter'd, as in a storm, to that harmonious breeze.
It floated now serenely, sweet of breath,
   As with full conscious beauty now content,
Now shivered into dim delicious death,
   Dash'd down a precipice of music, rent   10
By the mad stream of song; whirl'd, shook, rang out, spoke,
Stunning the charmed night with long melodies,
Then in a thousand gurgling eddies flew
   Of whirlwind sweetness, lost in its own sound,
As eddying winds of autumn when they blew,
   Caught the sere leaves and hurried round and round,
So her rich notes tumultuous panted she,
Then into fitful peace dropt down harmoniously.
Hark! now they storm again and whirl along
Swift passion; strange, passion should be so sweet!   20
What stings thee madly into sudden song,
   O nightingale? What joy or grief is meet
To father such delight? Some say for ever
Thy wild strain blindly maddens down grief's passion-river;
Others, that with fierce joy intoxicate
   Thou variest in sweet labyrinthine maze
A wild delight of thy rich woodland state
   Alone among green leaves, where softly plays
Thy trembling wooer, Zephyr; whatsoe'er
No grief or joy of ours was ever yet so fair.   30
Never but once did mortal fire of passion
   Such a fierce sweetness thrill, when she who died
Whirl'd by a storm of love and indignation
   From dusk Leucadia's rock, her poet pride
Mastering wild love, rung out her burning song

To Lemnos' shades and seas, her laurell'd troop among.
Never was sorrow half so full of joy,
    Never was joy so like her sister sorrow;
Yet twins they are, and to the nearing eye
    Alike inseparable, so one doth borrow   40
The other's eyes to look more beautiful,
And both with mingled voice thy cup of song make full.
Sing on! thou singest as in early times
    To Thracian forests in the accursed shade;
Sing on: thou singest as of early crimes. . . .

A Ballad of Life

I found in dreams a place of wind and flowers,
    Full of sweet trees and colour of glad grass,
    In midst whereof there was
A lady clothed like summer with sweet hours.
Her beauty, fervent as a fiery moon,
    Made my blood burn and swoon
        Like a flame rained upon.
Sorrow had filled her shaken eyelids' blue,
And her mouth's sad red heavy rose all through
        Seemed sad with glad things gone.   10

She held a little cithern by the strings,
    Shaped heartwise, strung with subtle-coloured hair
    Of some dead lute-player
That in dead years had done delicious things.
The seven strings were named accordingly;
    The first string charity,
        The second tenderness,
The rest were pleasure, sorrow, sleep, and sin,
And loving-kindness, that is pity's kin
        And is most pitiless.   20

There were three men with her, each garmented
    With gold and shod with gold upon the feet;

And with plucked ears of wheat
The first man's hair was wound upon his head:
His face was red, and his mouth curled and sad;
    All his gold garment had
      Pale stains of dust and rust.
A riven hood was pulled across his eyes;
The token of him being upon this wise
      Made for a sign of Lust.   30

The next was Shame, with hollow heavy face
    Coloured like green wood when flame kindles it.
    He hath such feeble feet
They may not well endure in any place.
His face was full of grey old miseries,
    And all his blood's increase
      Was even increase of pain.
The last was Fear, that is akin to Death;
He is Shame's friend, and always as Shame saith
      Fear answers him again.   40

My soul said in me; This is marvellous,
    Seeing the air's face is not so delicate
    Nor the sun's grace so great,
If sin and she be kin or amorous.
And seeing where maidens served her on their knees,
    I bade one crave of these
      To know the cause thereof.
Then Fear said: I am Pity that was dead.
And Shame said: I am Sorrow comforted.
      And Lust said: I am Love.   50

Thereat her hands began a lute-playing
    And her sweet mouth a song in a strange tongue;
    And all the while she sung
There was no sound but long tears following
Long tears upon men's faces, waxen white
    With extreme sad delight.
      But those three following men
Became as men raised up among the dead;

Great glad mouths open and fair cheeks made red
    With child's blood come again.   60

Then I said: Now assuredly I see
  My lady is perfect, and transfigureth
  All sin and sorrow and death,
Making them fair as her own eyelids be,
Or lips wherein my whole soul's life abides;
    Or as her sweet white sides
    And bosom carved to kiss.
Now therefore, if her pity further me,
Doubtless for her sake all my days shall be
    As righteous as she is.   70

Forth, ballad, and take roses in both arms,
  Even till the top rose touch thee in the throat
Where the least thornprick harms;
  And girdled in thy golden singing-coat,
Come thou before my lady and say this;
  Borgia, thy gold hair's colour burns in me,
    Thy mouth makes beat my blood in feverish rhymes;
  Therefore so many as these roses be,
    Kiss me so many times.
Then it may be, seeing how sweet she is,   80
  That she will stoop herself none otherwise
    Than a blown vine-branch doth,
And kiss thee with soft laughter on thine eyes,
    Ballad, and on thy mouth.

A Ballad of Death

  Kneel down, fair Love, and fill thyself with tears,
  Girdle thyself with sighing for a girth
  Upon the sides of mirth,
  Cover thy lips and eyelids, let thine ears
  Be filled with rumour of people sorrowing;

Make thee soft raiment out of woven sighs
Upon the flesh to cleave,
Set pains therein and many a grievous thing,
And many sorrows after each his wise
For armlet and for gorget and for sleeve.   10

O Love's lute heard about the lands of death,
Left hanged upon the trees that were therein;
O Love and Time and Sin,
Three singing mouths that mourn now underbreath,
Three lovers, each one evil spoken of;
O smitten lips wherethrough this voice of mine
Came softer with her praise;
Abide a little for our lady's love.
The kisses of her mouth were more than wine,
And more than peace the passage of her days.   20

O Love, thou knowest if she were good to see.
O Time, thou shalt not find in any land
Till, cast out of thine hand,
The sunlight and the moonlight fail from thee,
Another woman fashioned like as this.
O Sin, thou knowest that all thy shame in her
Was made a goodly thing;
Yea, she caught Shame and shamed him with her kiss,
With her fair kiss, and lips much lovelier
Than lips of amorous roses in late spring.   30

By night there stood over against my bed
Queen Venus with a hood striped gold and black,
Both sides drawn fully back
From brows wherein the sad blood failed of red,
And temples drained of purple and full of death.
Her curled hair had the wave of sea-water
And the sea's gold in it.
Her eyes were as a dove's that sickeneth.
Strewn dust of gold she had shed over her,
And pearl and purple and amber on her feet.   40

Upon her raiment of dyed sendaline
Were painted all the secret ways of love

And covered things thereof,
That hold delight as grape-flowers hold their wine;
Red mouths of maidens and red feet of doves,
And brides that kept within the bride-chamber
Their garment of soft shame,
And weeping faces of the wearied loves
That swoon in sleep and awake wearier,
With heat of lips and hair shed out like flame.   50

The tears that through her eyelids fell on me
Made mine own bitter where they ran between
As blood had fallen therein,
She saying; Arise, life up thine eyes and see
If any glad thing be or any good
Now the best thing is taken forth of us;
Even she to whom all praise
Was as one flower in a great multitude,
One glorious flower of many and glorious,
One day found gracious among many days: 60

Even she whose handmaiden was Love – to whom
At kissing times across her stateliest bed
Kings bowed themselves and shed
Pale wine, and honey with the honeycomb,
And spikenard bruised for a burnt-offering;
Even she between whose lips the kiss became
As fire and frankincense;
Whose hair was as gold raiment on a king,
Whose eyes were as the morning purged with flame,
Whose eyelids as sweet savour issuing thence.   70

Then I beheld, and lo on the other side
My lady's likeness crowned and robed and dead.
Sweet still, but now not red,
Was the shut mouth whereby men lived and died.
And sweet, but emptied of the blood's blue shade,
The great curled eyelids that withheld her eyes.
And sweet, but like spoilt gold,
The weight of colour in her tresses weighed.

And sweet, but as a vesture with new dyes,
The body that was clothed with love of old.   80

Ah! that my tears filled all her woven hair
And all the hollow bosom of her gown –
Ah! that my tears ran down
Even to the place where many kisses were,
Even where her parted breast-flowers have place,
Even where they are cloven apart – who knows not this?
Ah! the flowers cleave apart
And their sweet fills the tender interspace;
Ah! the leaves grown thereof were things to kiss
Ere their fine gold was tarnished at the heart.   90

Ah! in the days when God did good to me,
Each part about her was a righteous thing;
Her mouth an almsgiving,
The glory of her garments charity,
The beauty of her bosom a good deed,
In the good days when God kept sight of us;
Love lay upon her eyes,
And on that hair whereof the world takes heed;
And all her body was more virtuous
Than souls of women fashioned otherwise.   100

Now, ballad, gather poppies in thine hands
And sheaves of brier and many rusted sheaves
Rain-rotten in rank lands,
Waste marigold and late unhappy leaves
And grass that fades ere any of it be mown;
And when thy bosom is filled full thereof
Seek out Death's face ere the light altereth,
And say 'My master that was thrall to Love
Is become thrall to Death.'
Bow down before him, ballad, sigh and groan,   110
But make no sojourn in thy outgoing;
For haply it may be
That when thy feet return at evening
Death shall come in with thee.

The Triumph of Time

Before our lives divide for ever,
   While time is with us and hands are free,
(Time, swift to fasten and swift to sever
   Hand from hand, as we stand by the sea)
I will say no word that a man might say
Whose whole life's love goes down in a day;
For this could never have been; and never,
   Though the gods and the years relent, shall be.

Is it worth a tear, is it worth an hour,
   To think of things that are well outworn?   10
Of fruitless husk and fugitive flower,
   The dream foregone and the deed forborne?
Though joy be done with and grief be vain,
Time shall not sever us wholly in twain;
Earth is not spoilt for a single shower;
   But the rain has ruined the ungrown corn.

It will grow not again, this fruit of my heart,
   Smitten with sunbeams, ruined with rain.
The singing seasons divide and depart,
   Winter and summer depart in twain.   20
It will grow not again, it is ruined at root,
The bloodlike blossom, the dull red fruit;
Though the heart yet sickens, the lips yet smart,
   With sullen savour of poisonous pain.

I have given no man of my fruit to eat;
   I trod the grapes, I have drunken the wine.
Had you eaten and drunken and found it sweet,
   This wild new growth of the corn and vine,
This wine and bread without lees or leaven,
We had grown as gods, as the gods in heaven,   30
Souls fair to look upon, goodly to greet,
   One splendid spirit, your soul and mine.

In the change of years, in the coil of things,
   In the clamour and rumour of life to be,

We, drinking love at the furthest springs,
    Covered with love as a covering tree,
We had grown as gods, as the gods above,
Filled from the heart to the lips with love,
Held fast in his hands, clothed warm with his wings,
    O love, my love, had you loved but me!   40

We had stood as the sure stars stand, and moved
    As the moon moves, loving the world; and seen
Grief collapse as a thing disproved,
    Death consume as a thing unclean.
Twain halves of a perfect heart, made fast
Soul to soul while the years fell past;
Had you loved me once, as you have not loved;
    Had the chance been with us that has not been.

I have put my days and dreams out of mind,
    Days that are over, dreams that are done.   50
Though we seek life through, we shall surely find
    There is none of them clear to us now, not one.
But clear are these things; the grass and the sand,
Where, sure as the eyes reach, ever at hand,
With lips wide open and face burnt blind,
    The strong sea-daisies feast on the sun.

The low downs lean to the sea; the stream,
    One loose thin pulseless tremulous vein,
Rapid and vivid and dumb as a dream,
    Works downward, sick of the sun and the rain;   60
No wind is rough with the rank rare flowers;
The sweet sea, mother of loves and hours,
Shudders and shines as the grey winds gleam,
    Turning her smile to a fugitive pain.

Mother of loves that are swift to fade,
    Mother of mutable winds and hours.
A barren mother, a mother-maid,
    Cold and clean as her faint salt flowers.
I would we twain were even as she,

Lost in the night and the light of the sea,   70
Where faint sounds falter and wan beams wade,
   Break, and are broken, and shed into showers.

The loves and hours of the life of a man,
   They are swift and sad, being born of the sea.
Hours that rejoice and regret for a span,
   Born with a man's breath, mortal as he;
Loves that are lost ere they come to birth,
Weeds of the wave, without fruit upon earth.
I lose what I long for, save what I can,
   My love, my love, and no love for me!   80

It is not much that a man can save
   On the sands of life, in the straits of time,
Who swims in sight of the great third wave
   That never a swimmer shall cross or climb.
Some waif washed up with the strays and spars
That ebb-tide shows to the shore and the stars;
Weed from the water, grass from a grave,
   A broken blossom, a ruined rhyme.

There will no man do for your sake, I think,
   What I would have done for the least word said.   90
I had wrung life dry for your lips to drink,
   Broken it up for your daily bread:
Body for body and blood for blood,
As the flow of the full sea risen to flood
That yearns and trembles before it sink,
   I had given, and lain down for you, glad and dead.

Yea, hope at highest and all her fruit,
   And time at fullest and all his dower,
I had given you surely, and life to boot,
   Were we once made one for a single hour.   100
But now, you are twain, you are cloven apart,
Flesh of his flesh, but heart of my heart;
And deep in one is the bitter root,
   And sweet for one is the lifelong flower.

To have died if you cared I should die for you, clung
    To my life if you bade me, played my part
As it pleased you – these were the thoughts that stung,
    The dreams that smote with a keener dart
Than shafts of love or arrows of death;
These were but as fire is, dust, or breath,   110
Or poisonous foam on the tender tongue
    Of the little snakes that eat my heart.

I wish we were dead together today,
    Lost sight of, hidden away out of sight,
Clasped and clothed in the cloven clay,
    Out of the world's way, out of the light,
Out of the ages of worldly weather,
Forgotten of all men altogether,
As the world's first dead, taken wholly away,
    Made one with death, filled full of the night.   120

How we should slumber, how we should sleep,
    Far in the dark with the dreams and the dews!
And dreaming, grow to each other, and weep,
    Laugh low, live softly, murmur and muse;
Yea, and it may be, struck through by the dream,
Feel the dust quicken and quiver, and seem
Alive as of old to the lips, and leap
    Spirit to spirit as lovers use.

Sick dreams and sad of a dull delight;
    For what shall it profit when men are dead   130
    To have dreamed, to have loved with the whole soul's might,
    To have looked for day when the day was fled?
Let come what will, there is one thing worth,
To have had fair love in the life upon earth:
To have held love safe till the day grew night,
    While skies had colour and lips were red.

Would I lose you now? would I take you then,
    If I lose you now that my heart has need?
And come what may after death to men,

What thing worth this will the dead years breed?   140
Lose life, lose all; but at least I know,
O sweet life's love, having loved you so,
Had I reached you on earth, I should lose not again,
　In death nor life, nor in dream or deed.

Yea, I know this well: were you once sealed mine,
　Mine in the blood's beat, mine in the breath,
Mixed into me as honey in wine,
　Not time, that sayeth and gainsayeth,
Nor all strong things had severed us then;
Not wrath of gods, nor wisdom of men,   150
Nor all things earthly, nor all divine,
　Nor joy nor sorrow, nor life nor death.

I had grown pure as the dawn and the dew,
　You had grown strong as the sun or the sea.
But none shall triumph a whole life through:
　For death is one, and the fates are three.
At the door of life, by the gate of breath,
There are worse things waiting for men than death;
Death could not sever my soul and you,
　As these have severed your soul from me.   160

You have chosen and clung to the chance they sent you,
　Life sweet as perfume and pure as prayer.
But will it not one day in heaven repent you?
　Will they solace you wholly, the days that were?
Will you lift up your eyes between sadness and bliss,
Meet mine, and see where the great love is,
And tremble and turn and be changed? Content you;
　The gate is strait; I shall not be there.

But you, had you chosen, had you stretched hand,
　Had you seen good such a thing were done,   170
I too might have stood with the souls that stand
　In the sun's sight, clothed with the light of the sun;
But who now on earth need care how I live?
Have the high gods anything left to give,

Save dust and laurels and gold and sand?
   Which gifts are goodly; but I will none.

O all fair lovers about the world,
   There is none of you, none, that shall comfort me.
My thoughts are as dead things, wrecked and whirled
   Round and round in a gulf of the sea;   180
And still, through the sound and the straining stream,
Through the coil and chafe, they gleam in a dream,
The bright fine lips so cruelly curled,
   And strange swift eyes where the soul sits free.

Free, without pity, withheld from woe,
   Ignorant; fair as the eyes are fair.
Would I have you change now, change at a blow,
   Startled and stricken, awake and aware?
Yea, if I could, would I have you see
My very love of you filling me,   190
And know my soul to the quick, as I know
   The likeness and look of your throat and hair?

I shall not change you. Nay, though I might,
   Would I change my sweet one love with a word?
I had rather your hair should change in a night,
   Clear now as the plume of a black bright bird;
Your face fail suddenly, cease, turn grey,
Die as a leaf that dies in a day.
I will keep my soul in a place out of sight,
   Far off, where the pulse of it is not heard.   200

Far off it walks, in a bleak blown space,
   Full of the sound of the sorrow of years.
I have woven a veil for the weeping face,
   Whose lips have drunken the wine of tears;
I have found a way for the failing feet,
A place for slumber and sorrow to meet;
There is no rumour about the place,
   Nor light, nor any that sees or hears.

I have hidden my soul out of sight, and said
   'Let none take pity upon thee, none   210

Comfort thy crying: for lo, thou art dead,
  Lie still now, safe out of sight of the sun.
Have I not built thee a grave, and wrought
Thy grave-clothes on thee of grievous thought,
With soft spun verses and tears unshed,
  And sweet light visions of things undone?

'I have given thee garments and balm and myrrh,
  And gold, and beautiful burial things.
But thou, be at peace now, make no stir;
  Is not thy grave as a royal king's?   220
Fret not thyself though the end were sore;
Sleep, be patient, vex me no more.
Sleep; what hast thou to do with her?
  The eyes that weep, with the mouth that sings?'

Where the dead red leaves of the years lie rotten,
  The cold old crimes and the deeds thrown by,
The misconceived and the misbegotten,
  I would find a sin to do ere I die,
Sure to dissolve and destroy me all through,
That would set you higher in heaven, serve you   230
And leave you happy, when clean forgotten,
  As a dead man out of mind, am I.

Your lithe hands draw me, your face burns through me,
  I am swift to follow you, keen to see;
But love lacks might to redeem or undo me;
  As I have been, I know I shall surely be;
'What should such fellows as I do?' Nay,
My part were worse if I chose to play;
For the worst is this after all; if they knew me,
  Not a soul upon earth would pity me.   240

And I play not for pity of these; but you,
  If you saw with your soul what man am I,
You would praise me at least that my soul all through
  Clove to you, loathing the lives that lie;
The souls and lips that are bought and sold,
The smiles of silver and kisses of gold,

The lapdog loves that whine as they chew,
   The little lovers that curse and cry.

There are fairer women, I hear; that may be;
   But I, that I love you and find you fair,   250
Who are more than fair in my eyes if they be,
   Do the high gods know or the great gods care?
Though the swords in my heart for one were seven,
Would the iron hollow of doubtful heaven,
That knows not itself whether night-time or day be,
   Reverberate words and a foolish prayer?

I will go back to the great sweet mother,
   Mother and lover of men, the sea.
I will go down to her, I and none other,
   Close with her, kiss her and mix her with me;   260
Cling to her, strive with her, hold her fast:
O fair white mother, in days long past
Born without sister, born without brother,
   Set free my soul as thy soul is free.

A fair green-girdled mother of mine,
   Sea, that art clothed with the sun and the rain,
Thy sweet hard kisses are strong like wine,
   Thy large embraces are keen like pain.
Save me and hide me with all thy waves,
Find me one grave of thy thousand graves,   270
Those pure cold populous graves of thine
   Wrought without hand in a world without stain.

I shall sleep, and move with the moving ships,
   Change as the winds change, veer in the tide;
My lips will feast on the foam of thy lips,
   I shall rise with thy rising, with thee subside;
Sleep, and not know if she be, if she were,
Filled full with life to the eyes and hair,
As a rose is fulfilled to the roseleaf tips
   With splendid summer and perfume and pride.   280

This woven raiment of nights and days,
   Were it once cast off and unwound from me,

Naked and glad would I walk in thy ways,
    Alive and aware of thy ways and thee;
Clear of the whole world, hidden at home,
Clothed with the green and crowned with the foam,
A pulse of the life of thy straits and bays,
    A vein in the heart of the streams of the sea.

Fair mother, fed with the lives of men,
    Thou art subtle and cruel of heart, men say.   290
Thou hast taken, and shalt not render again;
    Thou art full of thy dead, and cold as they.
But death is the worst that comes of thee;
Thou art fed with our dead, O mother, O sea,
But when hast thou fed on our hearts? or when,
    Having given us love, hast thou taken away?

O tender-hearted, O perfect lover,
    Thy lips are bitter, and sweet thine heart.
The hopes that hurt and the dreams that hover,
    Shall they not vanish away and apart?   300
But thou, thou art sure, thou art older than earth;
Thou art strong for death and fruitful of birth;
Thy depths conceal and thy gulfs discover;
    From the first thou wert; in the end thou art.

And grief shall endure not for ever, I know.
    As things that are not shall these things be;
We shall live through seasons of sun and of snow,
    And none be grievous as this to me.
We shall hear, as one in a trance that hears,
The sound of time, the rhyme of the years;   310
Wrecked hope and passionate pain will grow
    As tender things of a spring-tide sea.

Sea-fruit that swings in the waves that hiss,
    Drowned gold and purple and royal rings.
And all time past, was it all for this?
    Times unforgotten, and treasures of things?
Swift years of liking and sweet long laughter,

That wist not well of the years thereafter
Till love woke, smitten at heart by a kiss,
   With lips that trembled and trailing wings?   320

There lived a singer in France of old
   By the tideless dolorous midland sea.
In a land of sand and ruin and gold
   There shone one woman, and none but she.
And finding life for her love's sake fail,
Being fain to see her, he bade set sail,
Touched land, and saw her as life grew cold,
   And praised God, seeing; and so died he.

Died, praising God for his gift and grace:
   For she bowed down to him weeping, and said   330
'Live'; and her tears were shed on his face
   Or ever the life in his face was shed.
The sharp tears fell through her hair, and stung
Once, and her close lips touched him and clung
Once, and grew one with his lips for a space;
   And so drew back, and the man was dead.

O brother, the gods were good to you.
   Sleep, and be glad while the world endures.
Be well content as the years wear through;
   Give thanks for life, and the loves and lures;   340
Give thanks for life, O brother, and death,
For the sweet last sound of her feet, her breath,
For gifts she gave you, gracious and few,
   Tears and kisses, that lady of yours.

Rest, and be glad of the gods; but I,
   How shall I praise them, or how take rest?
There is not room under all the sky
   For me that know not of worst or best,
Dream or desire of the days before,
Sweet things or bitterness, any more.   350
Love will not come to me now though I die,
   As love came close to you, breast to breast.

I shall never be friends again with roses;
   I shall loathe sweet tunes, where a note grown strong
Relents and recoils, and climbs and closes,
   As a wave of the sea turned back by song.
There are sounds where the soul's delight takes fire,
Face to face with its own desire;
A delight that rebels, a desire that reposes;
   I shall hate sweet music my whole life long.   360

The pulse of war and passion of wonder,
   The heavens that murmur, the sounds that shine,
The stars that sing and the loves that thunder,
   The music burning at heart like wine,
An armed archangel whose hands raise up
All senses mixed in the spirit's cup
Till flesh and spirit are molten in sunder –
   These things are over, and no more mine.

These were a part of the playing I heard
   Once, ere my love and my heart were at strife;   370
Love that sings and hath wings as a bird,
   Balm of the wound and heft of the knife.
Fairer than earth is the sea, and sleep
Than overwatching of eyes that weep,
Now time has done with his one sweet word,
   The wine and leaven of lovely life.

I shall go my ways, tread out my measure,
   Fill the days of my daily breath
With fugitive things not good to treasure,
   Do as the world doth, say as it saith;   380
But if we had loved each other – O sweet,
Had you felt, lying under the palms of your feet,
The heart of my heart, beating harder with pleasure
   To feel you tread it to dust and death –

Ah, had I not taken my life up and given
   All that life gives and the years let go,
The wine and honey, the balm and leaven,
   The dreams reared high and the hopes brought low?

Come life, come death, not a word be said;
   Should I lose you living, and vex you dead?   390
I never shall tell you on earth; and in heaven,
   If I cry to you then, will you hear or know?

Les Noyades

Whatever a man of the sons of men
   Shall say to his heart of the lords above,
They have shown man verily, once and again,
   Marvellous mercies and infinite love.

In the wild fifth year of the change of things,
   When France was glorious and blood-red, fair
With dust of battle and deaths of kings,
   A queen of men, with helmeted hair,

Carrier came down to the Loire and slew,
   Till all the ways and the waves waxed red: 10
Bound and drowned, slaying two by two,
   Maidens and young men, naked and wed.

They brought on a day to his judgment-place
   One rough with labour and red with fight,
And a lady noble by name and face,
   Faultless, a maiden, wonderful, white.

She knew not, being for shame's sake blind,
   If his eyes were hot on her face hard by.
And the judge bade strip and ship them, and bind
   Bosom to bosom, to drown and die.   20

The white girl winced and whitened; but he
   Caught fire, waxed bright as a great bright flame
Seen with thunder far out on the sea,
   Laughed hard as the glad blood went and came.

Twice his lips quailed with delight, then said,
   'I have but a word to you all, one word;
Bear with me; surely I am but dead;'
   And all they laughed and mocked him and heard.

'Judge, when they open the judgment-roll,
   I will stand upright before God and pray: 30
"Lord God, have mercy on one man's soul,
   For his mercy was great upon earth, I say.

' "Lord, if I loved thee – Lord, if I served –
   If these who darkened thy fair Son's face
I fought with, sparing not one, nor swerved
   A hand's-breadth, Lord, in the perilous place –

' "I pray thee say to this man, O Lord,
   Sit thou for him at my feet on a throne.
I will face thy wrath, though it bite as a sword,
   And my soul shall burn for his soul, and atone.   40

' "For, Lord, thou knowest, O God most wise,
   How gracious on earth were his deeds towards me.
Shall this be a small thing in thine eyes,
   That is greater in mine than the whole great sea?"

'I have loved this woman my whole life long,
   And even for love's sake when have I said
"I love you"? when have I done you wrong,
   Living? but now I shall have you dead.

'Yea, now, do I bid you love me, love?
   Love me or loathe, we are one not twain.   50
But God be praised in his heaven above
   For this my pleasure and that my pain!

'For never a man, being mean like me,
   Shall die like me till the whole world dies.
I shall drown with her, laughing for love; and she
   Mix with me, touching me, lips and eyes.

'Shall she not know me and see me all through,
 Me, on whose heart as a worm she trod?
You have given me, God requite it you,
 What man yet never was given of God.'   60

O sweet one love, O my life's delight,
 Dear, though the days have divided us,
Lost beyond hope, taken far out of sight,
 Not twice in the world shall the gods do thus.

Had it been so hard for my love? but I,
 Though the gods gave all that a god can give,
I had chosen rather the gift to die,
 Cease, and be glad above all that live.

For the Loire would have driven us down to the sea,
 And the sea would have pitched us from shoal to shoal; 70
And I should have held you, and you held me,
 As flesh holds flesh, and the soul the soul.

Could I change you, help you to love me, sweet,
 Could I give you the love that would sweeten death,
We should yield, go down, locked hands and feet,
 Die, drown together, and breath catch breath;

But you would have felt my soul in a kiss,
 And known that once if I loved you well;
And I would have given my soul for this
 To burn for ever in burning hell.   80

Itylus

Swallow, my sister, O sister swallow,
 How can thine heart be full of the spring?
  A thousand summers are over and dead.
What hast thou found in the spring to follow?

What hast thou found in thine heart to sing?
    What wilt thou do when the summer is shed?

O swallow, sister, O fair swift swallow,
    Why wilt thou fly after spring to the south,
        The soft south whither thine heart is set?
Shall not the grief of the old time follow?   10
    Shall not the song thereof cleave to thy mouth?
        Hast thou forgotten ere I forget?

Sister, my sister, O fleet sweet swallow,
    Thy way is long to the sun and the south;
        But I, fulfilled of my heart's desire,
Shedding my song upon height, upon hollow,
    From tawny body and sweet small mouth
        Feed the heart of the night with fire.

I the nightingale all spring through,
    A swallow, sister, O changing swallow,   20
        All spring through till the spring be done,
Clothed with the light of the night on the dew,
    Sing, while the hours and the wild birds follow,
        Take flight and follow and find the sun.

Sister, my sister, O soft light swallow,
    Though all things feast in the spring's guest-chamber,
        How hast thou heart to be glad thereof yet?
For where thou fliest I shall not follow,
    Till life forget and death remember,
        Till thou remember and I forget.   30

Swallow, my sister, O singing swallow,
    I know not how thou hast heart to sing.
        Hast thou the heart? is it all past over?
Thy lord the summer is good to follow,
    And fair the feet of thy lover the spring:
        But what wilt thou say to the spring thy lover?

O swallow, sister, O fleeting swallow,
    My heart in me is a molten ember

And over my head the waves have met.
But thou wouldst tarry or I would follow,   40
  Could I forget or thou remember,
    Couldst thou remember and I forget.

O sweet stray sister, O shifting swallow,
  The heart's division divideth us.
    Thy heart is light as a leaf of a tree;
But mine goes forth among sea-gulfs hollow
  To the place of the slaying of Itylus,
    The feast of Daulis, the Thracian sea.

O swallow, sister, O rapid swallow,
  I pray thee sing not a little space.   50
    Are not the roofs and the lintels wet?
The woven web that was plain to follow,
  The small slain body, the flowerlike face,
    Can I remember if thou forget?

O sister, sister, thy first-begotten!
  The hands that cling and the feet that follow,
  The voice of the child's blood crying yet
Who hath remembered me? who hath forgotten?
  Thou hast forgotten, O summer swallow,
    But the world shall end when I forget.   60

Anactoria

τίνος αὖ τὺ πειθοῖ.
μὰψ σαγηνεύσας φιλότατα;
SAPPHO

My life is bitter with thy love; thine eyes
Blind me, thy tresses burn me, thy sharp sighs
Divide my flesh and spirit with soft sound,
And my blood strengthens, and my veins abound.
I pray thee sigh not, speak not, draw not breath;

Let life burn down, and dream it is not death.
I would the sea had hidden us, the fire
(Wilt thou fear that, and fear not my desire?)
Severed the bones that bleach, the flesh that cleaves,
And let our sifted ashes drop like leaves.   10
I feel thy blood against my blood: my pain
Pains thee, and lips bruise lips, and vein stings vein.
Let fruit be crushed on fruit, let flower on flower,
Breast kindle breast, and either burn one hour.
Why wilt thou follow lesser loves? are thine
Too weak to bear these hands and lips of mine?
I charge thee for my life's sake, O too sweet
To crush love with thy cruel faultless feet,
I charge thee keep thy lips from hers or his,
Sweetest, till theirs be sweeter than my kiss: 20
Lest I too lure, a swallow for a dove,
Erotion or Erinna to my love.
I would my love could kill thee; I am satiated
With seeing thee live, and fain would have thee dead.
I would earth had thy body as fruit to eat,
And no mouth but some serpent's found thee sweet.
I would find grievous ways to have thee slain,
Intense device, and superflux of pain;
Vex thee with amorous agonies, and shake
Life at thy lips, and leave it there to ache;   30
Strain out thy soul with pangs too soft to kill,
Intolerable interludes, and infinite ill;
Relapse and reluctation of the breath,
Dumb tunes and shuddering semitones of death.
I am weary of all thy words and soft strange ways,
Of all love's fiery nights and all his days,
And all the broken kisses salt as brine
That shuddering lips make moist with waterish wine,
And eyes the bluer for all those hidden hours
That pleasure fills with tears and feeds from flowers,   40
Fierce at the heart with fire that half comes through,
But all the flowerlike white stained round with blue;
The fervent underlid, and that above
Lifted with laughter or abashed with love;
Thine amorous girdle, full of thee and fair,

And leavings of the lilies in thine hair.
Yea, all sweet words of thine and all thy ways,
And all the fruit of nights and flower of days,
And stinging lips wherein the hot sweet brine
That Love was born of burns and foams like wine,   50
And eyes insatiable of amorous hours,
Fervent as fire and delicate as flowers,
Coloured like night at heart, but cloven through
Like night with flame, dyed round like night with blue,
Clothed with deep eyelids under and above –
Yea, all thy beauty sickens me with love;
Thy girdle empty of thee and now not fair,
And ruinous lilies in thy languid hair.
Ah, take no thought for Love's sake; shall this be,
And she who loves thy lover not love thee?   60
Sweet soul, sweet mouth of all that laughs and lives,
Mine is she, very mine; and she forgives.
For I beheld in sleep the light that is
In her high place in Paphos, heard the kiss
Of body and soul that mix with eager tears
And laughter stinging through the eyes and ears;
Saw Love, as burning flame from crown to feet,
Imperishable, upon her storied seat;
Clear eyelids lifted toward the north and south,
A mind of many colours, and a mouth   70
Of many tunes and kisses; and she bowed,
With all her subtle face laughing aloud,
Bowed down upon me, saying, 'Who doth thee wrong,
Sappho?' but thou – thy body is the song,
Thy mouth the music; thou art more than I,
Though my voice die not till the whole world die;
Though men that hear it madden; though love weep,
Though nature change, though shame be charmed to sleep.
Ah, wilt thou slay me lest I kiss thee dead?
Yet the queen laughed from her sweet heart and said: 80
'Even she that flies shall follow for thy sake,
And she shall give thee gifts that would not take,
Shall kiss that would not kiss thee' (yea, kiss me)
'When thou wouldst not' – when I would not kiss thee!
Ah, more to me than all men as thou art,

Shall not my songs assuage her at the heart?
Ah, sweet to me as life seems sweet to death,
Why should her wrath fill thee with fearful breath?
Nay, sweet, for is she God alone? hath she
Made earth and all the centuries of the sea,   90
Taught the sun ways to travel, woven most fine
The moonbeams, shed the starbeams forth as wine,
Bound with her myrtles, beaten with her rods,
The young men and the maidens and the gods?
Have we not lips to love with, eyes for tears,
And summer and flower of women and of years?
Stars for the foot of morning, and for noon
Sunlight, and exaltation of the moon;
Waters that answer waters, fields that wear
Lilies, and languor of the Lesbian air?   100
Beyond those flying feet of fluttered doves,
Are there not other gods for other loves?
Yea, though she scourge thee, sweetest, for my sake,
Blossom not thorns and flowers not blood should break.
Ah that my lips were tuneless lips, but pressed
To the bruised blossom of thy scourged white breast!
Ah that my mouth for Muses' milk were fed
On the sweet blood thy sweet small wounds had bled!
That with my tongue I felt them, and could taste
The faint flakes from thy bosom to the waist!   110
That I could drink thy veins as wine, and eat
Thy breasts like honey! that from face to feet
Thy body were abolished and consumed,
And in my flesh thy very flesh entombed!
Ah, ah, thy beauty! like a beast it bites,
Stings like an adder, like an arrow smites.
Ah sweet, and sweet again, and seven times sweet,
The paces and the pauses of thy feet!
Ah sweeter than all sleep or summer air
The fallen fillets fragrant from thine hair!   120
Yea, though their alien kisses do me wrong,
Sweeter thy lips than mine with all their song;
Thy shoulders whiter than a fleece of white,
And flower-sweet fingers, good to bruise or bite
As honeycomb of the inmost honey-cells,

With almond-shaped and roseleaf-coloured shells
And blood like purple blossom at the tips
Quivering; and pain made perfect in thy lips
For my sake when I hurt thee; O that I
Durst crush thee out of life with love, and die,   130
Die of thy pain and my delight, and be
Mixed with thy blood and molten into thee!
Would I not plague thee dying overmuch?
Would I not hurt thee perfectly? not touch
Thy pores of sense with torture, and make bright
Thine eyes with bloodlike tears and grievous light?
Strike pang from pang as note is struck from note,
Catch the sob's middle music in thy throat,
Take thy limbs living, and new-mould with these
A lyre of many faultless agonies?   140
Feed thee with fever and famine and fine drouth,
With perfect pangs convulse thy perfect mouth,
Make thy life shudder in thee and burn afresh,
And wring thy very spirit through the flesh?
Cruel? but love makes all that love him well
As wise as heaven and crueller than hell.
Me hath love made more bitter toward thee
Than death toward man; but were I made as he
Who hath made all things to break them one by one,
If my feet trod upon the stars and sun   150
And souls of men as his have alway trod,
God knows I might be crueller than God.
For who shall change with prayers or thanksgivings
The mystery of the cruelty of things?
Or say what God above all gods and years
With offering and blood-sacrifice of tears,
With lamentation from strange lands, from graves
Where the snake pastures, from scarred mouths of slaves,
From prison, and from plunging prows of ships
Through flamelike foam of the sea's closing lips –   160
With thwartings of strange signs, and wind-blown hair
Of comets, desolating the dim air,
When darkness is made fast with seals and bars,
And fierce reluctance of disastrous stars,
Eclipse, and sound of shaken hills, and wings

Darkening, and blind inexpiable things –
With sorrow of labouring moons, and altering light
And travail of the planets of the night,
And weeping of the weary Pleiads seven,
Feeds the mute melancholy lust of heaven? 170
Is not his incense bitterness, his meat
Murder? his hidden face and iron feet
Hath not man known, and felt them on their way
Threaten and trample all things and every day?
Hath he not sent us hunger? who hath cursed
Spirit and flesh with longing? filled with thirst
Their lips who cried unto him? who bade exceed
The fervid will, fall short the feeble deed,
Bade sink the spirit and the flesh aspire,
Pain animate the dust of dead desire, 180
And life yield up her flower to violent fate?
Him would I reach, him smite, him desecrate,
Pierce the cold lips of God with human breath,
And mix his immortality with death.
Why hath he made us? what had all we done
That we should live and loathe the sterile sun,
And with the moon wax paler as she wanes,
And pulse by pulse feel time grow through our veins?
Thee too the years shall cover; thou shalt be
As the rose born of one same blood with thee, 190
As a song sung, as a word said, and fall
Flower-wise, and be not any more at all,
Nor any memory of thee anywhere;
For never Muse has bound above thine hair
The high Pierian flower whose graft outgrows
All summer kinship of the mortal rose
And colour of deciduous days, nor shed
Reflex and flush of heaven above thine head,
Nor reddened brows made pale by floral grief
With splendid shadow from that lordlier leaf. 200
Yea, thou shalt be forgotten like spilt wine,
Except these kisses of my lips on thine
Brand them with immortality; but me –
Men shall not see bright fire nor hear the sea,
Nor mix their hearts with music, nor behold

Cast forth of heaven, with feet of awful gold
And plumeless wings that make the bright air blind,
Lightning, with thunder for a hound behind
Hunting through fields unfurrowed and unsown,
But in the light and laughter, in the moan   210
And music, and in grasp of lip and hand
And shudder of water that makes felt on land
The immeasurable tremor of all the sea,
Memories shall mix and metaphors of me.
Like me shall be the shuddering calm of night,
When all the winds of the world for pure delight
Close lips that quiver and fold up wings that ache;
When nightingales are louder for love's sake,
And leaves tremble like lute-strings or like fire;
Like me the one star swooning with desire   220
Even at the cold lips of the sleepless moon,
As I at thine; like me the waste white noon,
Burnt through with barren sunlight; and like me
The land-stream and the tide-stream in the sea.
I am sick with time as these with ebb and flow,
And by the yearning in my veins I know
The yearning sound of waters; and mine eyes
Burn as that beamless fire which fills the skies
With troubled stars and travailing things of flame;
And in my heart the grief consuming them   230
Labours, and in my veins the thirst of these,
And all the summer travail of the trees
And all the winter sickness; and the earth,
Filled full with deadly works of death and birth,
Sore spent with hungry lusts of birth and death,
Has pain like mine in her divided breath;
Her spring of leaves is barren, and her fruit
Ashes; her boughs are burdened, and her root
Fibrous and gnarled with poison; underneath
Serpents have gnawn it through with tortuous teeth   240
Made sharp upon the bones of all the dead,
And wild birds rend her branches overhead.
These, woven as raiment for his word and thought,
These hath God made, and me as these, and wrought
Song, and hath lit it at my lips; and me

Earth shall not gather though she feed on thee.
As a shed tear shalt thou be shed; but I –
Lo, earth may labour, men live long and die,
Years change and stars, and the high God devise
New things, and old things wane before his eyes   250
Who wields and wrecks them, being more strong than they –
But, having made me, me he shall not slay.
Nor slay nor satiate, like those herds of his
Who laugh and live a little, and their kiss
Contents them, and their loves are swift and sweet,
And sure death grasps and gains them with slow feet,
Love they or hate they, strive or bow their knees –
And all these end; he hath his will of these.
Yea, but albeit he slay me, hating me –
Albeit he hide me in the deep dear sea   260
And cover me with cool wan foam, and ease
This soul of mine as any soul of these,
And give me water and great sweet waves, and make
The very sea's name lordlier for my sake,
The whole sea sweeter – albeit I die indeed
And hide myself and sleep and no man heed,
Of me the high God hath not all his will.
Blossom of branches, and on each high hill
Clear air and wind, and under in clamorous vales
Fierce noises of the fiery nightingales,   270
Buds burning in the sudden spring like fire,
The wan washed sand and the waves' vain desire,
Sails seen like blown white flowers at sea, and words
That bring tears swiftest, and long notes of birds
Violently singing till the whole world sings –
I Sappho shall be one with all these things,
With all high things for ever; and my face
Seen once, my songs once heard in a strange place,
Cleave to men's lives, and waste the days thereof
With gladness and much sadness and long love.   280
Yea, they shall say, earth's womb has borne in vain
New things, and never this best thing again;
Borne days and men, borne fruits and wars and wine,
Seasons and songs, but no song more like mine.
And they shall know me as ye who have known me here,

Last year when I loved Atthis, and this year
When I love thee; and they shall praise me, and say
'She hath all time as all we have our day,
Shall she not live and have her will' – even I?
Yea, though thou diest, I say I shall not die.   290
For these shall give me of their souls, shall give
Life, and the days and loves wherewith I live,
Shall quicken me with loving, fill with breath,
Save me and serve me, strive for me with death.
Alas, that neither moon nor snow nor dew
Nor all cold things can purge me wholly through,
Assuage me nor allay me nor appease,
Till supreme sleep shall bring me bloodless ease;
Till time wax faint in all his periods;
Till fate undo the bondage of the gods,   300
And lay, to slake and satiate me all through,
Lotus and Lethe on my lips like dew,
And shed around and over and under me
Thick darkness and the insuperable sea.

Hermaphroditus

I

Lift up thy lips, turn round, look back for love,
   Blind love that comes by night and casts out rest;
   Of all things tired thy lips look weariest,
Save the long smile that they are wearied of.
Ah sweet, albeit no love be sweet enough,
   Choose of two loves and cleave unto the best;
   Two loves at either blossom of thy breast
Strive until one be under and one above.
Their breath is fire upon the amorous air,
   Fire in thine eyes and where thy lips suspire: 10
And whosoever hath seen thee, being so fair,
   Two things turn all his life and blood to fire;

A strong desire begot on great despair,
   A great despair cast out by strong desire.

             II

Where between sleep and life some brief space is,
   With love like gold bound round about the head,
   Sex to sweet sex with lips and limbs is wed,
Turning the fruitful feud of hers and his
To the waste wedlock of a sterile kiss;
   Yet from them something like as fire is shed   20
   That shall not be assuaged till death be dead,
Though neither life nor sleep can find out this.
Love made himself of flesh that perisheth
   A pleasure-house for all the loves his kin;
But on the one side sat a man like death,
   And on the other a woman sat like sin.
So with veiled eyes and sobs between his breath
   Love turned himself and would not enter in.

            III

Love, is it love or sleep or shadow or light
   That lies between thine eyelids and thine eyes?   30
   Like a flower laid upon a flower it lies,
Or like the night's dew laid upon the night.
Love stands upon thy left hand and thy right,
   Yet by no sunset and by no moonrise
   Shall make thee man and ease a woman's sighs,
Or make thee woman for a man's delight.
To what strange end hath some strange god made fair
   The double blossom of two fruitless flowers?
Hid love in all the folds of all thy hair,
   Fed thee on summers, watered thee with showers,   40
Given all the gold that all the seasons wear
   To thee that art a thing of barren hours?

            IV

Yea, love, I see; it is not love but fear.
   Nay, sweet, it is not fear but love, I know;
   Or wherefore should thy body's blossom blow
So sweetly, or thine eyelids leave so clear
Thy gracious eyes that never made a tear –

Though for their love our tears like blood should flow,
   Though love and life and death should come and go,
So dreadful, so desirable, so dear?   50
Yea, sweet, I know; I saw in what swift wise
   Beneath the woman's and the water's kiss
   Thy moist limbs melted into Salmacis,
And the large light turned tender in thine eyes,
And all thy boy's breath softened into sighs;
   But Love being blind, how should he know of this?

Au Musée du Louvre, Mars 1863

Fragoletta

O Love! what shall be said of thee?
The son of grief begot by joy?
Being sightless, wilt thou see?
Being sexless, wilt thou be
Maiden or boy?

I dreamed of strange lips yesterday
And cheeks wherein the ambiguous blood
Was like a rose's – yea,
A rose's when it lay
Within the bud.   10

What fields have bred thee, or what groves
Concealed thee, O mysterious flower,
O double rose of Love's,
With leaves that lure the doves
From bud to bower?

I dare not kiss it, lest my lip
Press harder than an indrawn breath,
And all the sweet life slip

Forth, and the sweet leaves drip,
Bloodlike, in death.   20

O sole desire of my delight!
O sole delight of my desire!
Mine eyelids and eyesight
Feed on thee day and night
Like lips of fire.

Lean back thy throat of carven pearl,
Let thy mouth murmur like the dove's;
Say, Venus hath no girl,
No front of female curl,
Among her Loves.   30

Thy sweet low bosom, thy close hair,
Thy strait soft flanks and slenderer feet,
Thy virginal strange air,
Are these not over fair
For Love to greet?

How should he greet thee? what new name,
Fit to move all men's hearts, could move
Thee, deaf to love or shame,
Love's sister, by the same
Mother as Love?   40

Ah sweet, the maiden's mouth is cold,
Her breast-blossoms are simply red,
Her hair mere brown or gold,
Fold over simple fold
Binding her head.

Thy mouth is made of fire and wine,
Thy barren bosom takes my kiss
And turns my soul to thine
And turns thy lips to mine,
And mine it is.   50

Thou hast a serpent in thine hair,
In all the curls that close and cling:

And ah, thy breast-flower!
Ah love, thy mouth too fair
To kiss and sting!

Cleave to me, love me, kiss mine eyes,
Satiate thy lips with loving me;
Nay, for thou shalt not rise;
Lie still as Love that dies
For love of thee.   60

Mine arms are close about thine head,
My lips are fervent on thy face,
And where my kiss hath fed
Thy flower-like blood leaps red
To the kissed place.

O bitterness of things too sweet!
O broken singing of the dove!
Love's wings are over fleet,
And like the panther's feet
The feet of Love.   70

Anima Anceps

Till death have broken
Sweet life's love-token,
Till all be spoken
    That shall be said,
What dost thou praying,
O soul, and playing
With song and saying,
    Things flown and fled?
For this we know not –
That fresh springs flow not   10
 And fresh griefs grow not
    When men are dead;

When strange years cover
Lover and lover,
And joys are over
   And tears are shed.

If one day's sorrow
Mar the day's morrow –
If man's life borrow
   And man's death pay –   20
If souls once taken,
If lives once shaken,
Arise, awaken,
   By night, by day –
Why with strong crying
And years of sighing,
Living and dying,
   Fast ye and pray?
For all your weeping,
Waking and sleeping,   30
Death comes to reaping
   And takes away.

Though time rend after
Roof-tree from rafter,
A little laughter
   Is much more worth
Than thus to measure
The hour, the treasure,
The pain, the pleasure,
   The death, the birth;   40
Grief, when days alter,
Like joy shall falter;
Song-book and psalter,
   Mourning and mirth.
Live like the swallow;
Seek not to follow
Where earth is hollow
   Under the earth.

In the Orchard

(Provençal Burden)

Leave go my hands, let me catch breath and see;
Let the dew-fall drench either side of me;
   Clear apple-leaves are soft upon that moon
Seen sidelong like a blossom in the tree;
   Ah God, ah God, that day should be so soon.

The grass is thick and cool, it lets us lie.
Kissed upon either cheek and either eye,
   I turn to thee as some green afternoon
Turns toward sunset, and is loth to die;
   Ah God, ah God, that day should be so soon.   10

Lie closer, lean your face upon my side,
Feel where the dew fell that has hardly dried,
   Hear how the blood beats that went nigh to swoon;
The pleasure lives there when the sense has died;
   Ah God, ah God, that day should be so soon.

O my fair lord, I charge you leave me this:
Is it not sweeter than a foolish kiss?
   Nay take it then, my flower, my first in June,
My rose, so like a tender mouth it is:
   Ah God, ah God, that day should be so soon.   20

Love, till dawn sunder night from day with fire,
Dividing my delight and my desire,
   The crescent life and love the plenilune,
Love me though dusk begin and dark retire;
   Ah God, ah God, that day should be so soon.

Ah, my heart fails, my blood draws back; I know,
When life runs over, life is near to go;
   And with the slain of love love's ways are strewn,

And with their blood, if love will have it so;
   Ah God, ah God, that day should be so soon.   30

Ah, do thy will now; slay me if thou wilt;
There is no building now the walls are built,
   No quarrying now the corner-stone is hewn,
No drinking now the vine's whole blood is spilt;
   Ah God, ah God, that day should be so soon.

Nay, slay me now; nay, for I will be slain;
Pluck thy red pleasure from the teeth of pain,
   Break down thy vine ere yet grape-gatherers prune,
Slay me ere day can slay desire again;
   Ah God, ah God, that day should be so soon.   40

Yea, with thy sweet lips, with thy sweet sword; yea,
Take life and all, for I will die, I say;
   Love, I gave love, is life a better boon?
For sweet night's sake I will not live till day;
   Ah God, ah God, that day should be so soon.

Nay, I will sleep then only; nay, but go.
Ah sweet, too sweet to me, my sweet, I know
   Love, sleep, and death go to the sweet same tune;
Hold my hair fast, and kiss me through it so.
   Ah God, ah God, that day should be so soon.   50

The Leper

Nothing is better, I well think,
   Than love; the hidden well-water
Is not so delicate to drink:
This was well seen of me and her.

I served her in a royal house;
   I served her wine and curious meat.

For will to kiss between her brows,
    I had no heart to sleep or eat.

Mere scorn God knows she had of me,
    A poor scribe, nowise great or fair,   10
Who plucked his clerk's hood back to see
    Her curled-up lips and amorous hair.

I vex my head with thinking this.
    Yea, though God always hated me,
And hates me now that I can kiss
    Her eyes, plait up her hair to see

How she then wore it on the brows,
    Yet am I glad to have her dead
Here in this wretched wattled house
    Where I can kiss her eyes and head.   20

Nothing is better, I well know,
    Than love; no amber in cold sea
Or gathered berries under snow:
    That is well seen of her and me.

Three thoughts I make my pleasure of:
    First I take heart and think of this:
That knight's gold hair she chose to love,
    His mouth she had such will to kiss.

Then I remember that sundawn
    I brought him by a privy way   30
Out at her lattice, and thereon
    What gracious words she found to say.

(Cold rushes for such little feet –
    Both feet could lie into my hand.
A marvel was it of my sweet
    Her upright body could so stand.)

'Sweet friend, God give you thank and grace;
    Now am I clean and whole of shame,

Nor shall men burn me in the face
    For my sweet fault that scandals them.'   40

I tell you over word by word.
    She, sitting edgewise on her bed,
Holding her feet, said thus. The third,
    A sweeter thing than these, I said.

God, that makes time and ruins it
    And alters not, abiding God,
Changed with disease her body sweet,
    The body of love wherein she abode.

Love is more sweet and comelier
    Than a dove's throat strained out to sing.   50
All they spat out and cursed at her
    And cast her forth for a base thing.

They cursed her, seeing how God had wrought
    This curse to plague her, a curse of his.
Fools were they surely, seeing not
    How sweeter than all sweet she is.

He that had held her by the hair,
    With kissing lips blinding her eyes,
Felt her bright bosom, strained and bare,
    Sigh under him, with short mad cries   60

Out of her throat and sobbing mouth
    And body broken up with love,
With sweet hot tears his lips were loth
    Her own should taste the savour of,

Yea, he inside whose grasp all night
    Her fervent body leapt or lay,
Stained with sharp kisses red and white,
    Found her a plague to spurn away.

I hid her in this wattled house,
    I served her water and poor bread.   70

For joy to kiss between her brows
　　Time upon time I was nigh dead.

Bread failed; we got but well-water
　　And gathered grass with dropping seed.
I had such joy of kissing her,
　　I had small care to sleep or feed.

Sometimes when service made me glad
　　The sharp tears leapt between my lids,
Falling on her, such joy I had
　　To do the service God forbids.　　　　　　80

'I pray you let me be at peace,
　　Get hence, make room for me to die.'
She said that: her poor lip would cease,
　　Put up to mine, and turn to cry.

I said, 'Bethink yourself how love
　　Fared in us twain, what either did;
Shall I unclothe my soul thereof?
　　That I should do this, God forbid.'

Yea, though God hateth us, he knows
　　That hardly in a little thing　　　　　　90
Love faileth of the work it does
　　Till it grow ripe for gathering.

Six months, and now my sweet is dead
　　A trouble takes me; I know not
If all were done well, all well said,
　　No word or tender deed forgot.

Too sweet, for the least part in her,
　　To have shed life out by fragments; yet,
Could the close mouth catch breath and stir,
　　I might see something I forget.　　　　　　100

Six months, and I sit still and hold
　　In two cold palms her cold two feet.

Her hair, half grey half ruined gold,
  Thrills me and burns me in kissing it.

Love bites and stings me through, to see
  Her keen face made of sunken bones.
Her worn-off eyelids madden me,
  That were shot through with purple once.

She said, 'Be good with me; I grow
  So tired for shame's sake, I shall die   110
If you say nothing': even so.
  And she is dead now, and shame put by.

Yea, and the scorn she had of me
  In the old time, doubtless vexed her then.
I never should have kissed her. See
  What fools God's anger makes of men!

She might have loved me a little too,
  Had I been humbler for her sake.
But that new shame could make love new
  She saw not – yet her shame did make.   120

I took too much upon my love,
  Having for such mean service done
Her beauty and all the ways thereof,
  Her face and all the sweet thereon.

Yea, all this while I tended her,
  I know the old love held fast his part:
I know the old scorn waxed heavier,
  Mixed with sad wonder, in her heart.

It may be all my love went wrong –
  A scribe's work writ awry and blurred,   130
Scrawled after the blind evensong –
  Spoilt music with no perfect word.

But surely I would fain have done
  All things the best I could. Perchance

Because I failed, came short of one,
  She kept at heart that other man's.

I am grown blind with all these things:
  It may be now she hath in sight
Some better knowledge; still there clings
  The old question. Will not God do right?*   140

Rondel

Kissing her hair I sat against her feet,
Wove and unwove it, wound and found it sweet;
Made fast therewith her hands, drew down her eyes,
Deep as deep flowers and dreamy like dim skies;
With her own tresses bound and found her fair,
  Kissing her hair.

* En ce temps-là estoyt dans ce pays grand nombre de ladres et de meseaulx, ce
dont le roy eut grand desplaisir, veu que Dieu dust en estre moult griefvement
courroucé. Ores il advint qu'une noble damoyselle appelée Yolande de Sallières
estant atteincte et touste guastée de ce vilain mal, tous ses amys et ses parens
ayant devant leurs yeux la paour de Dieu la firent issir fors de leurs maisons et
oncques ne voulurent recepvoir ni reconforter chose mauldicte de Dieu et à tous
les hommes puante et abhominable. Ceste dame avoyt esté moult belle et gracieuse
de formes, et de son corps elle estoyt large et de vie lascive. Pourtant nul des amans
qui l'avoyent souventesfois accollée et baisée moult tendrement ne voulust plus
héberger si laide femme et si détestable pescheresse. Ung seul clerc qui feut
premièrement son lacquays et son entremetteur en matière d'amour la reçut chez
luy et la récéla dans une petite cabane. Là mourut la meschinette de grande misère
et de male mort: et après elle décéda ledist clerc qui pour grand amour l'avoyt six
mois durant soignée, lavée, habillée et deshabillée tous les jours de ses mains
propres. Mesme dist-on que ce meschant homme et mauldict clerc se
remémourant de la grande beauté passée et guastée de ceste femme se délectoyt
maintesfois à la baiser sur sa bouche orde et lépreuse et l'accoller doulcement de
ses mains amoureuses. Aussy est-il mort de ceste mesme maladie abhominable.
Cecy advint près Fontainebellant en Gastinois. Et quand ouyt le roy Philippe ceste
adventure moult en estoyt esmerveillé.

Grandes Chroniques de France, 1505

Sleep were no sweeter than her face to me,
Sleep of cold sea-bloom under the cold sea;
What pain could get between my face and hers?
What new sweet thing would love not relish worse?
Unless, perhaps, white death had kissed me there,
   Kissing her hair?

Before the Mirror

(Verses Written Under a Picture)

Inscribed to J. A. Whistler

I

White rose in red rose-garden
  Is not so white;
Snowdrops that plead for pardon
  And pine for fright
Because the hard East blows
Over their maiden rows
  Grow not as this face grows from pale to bright.

Behind the veil, forbidden,
  Shut up from sight,
Love, is there sorrow hidden,
  Is there delight?
Is joy thy dower or grief,
White rose of weary leaf,
  Late rose whose life is brief, whose loves are light?

Soft snows that hard winds harden
  Till each flake bite
Fill all the flowerless garden
  Whose flowers took flight
Long since when summer ceased,
And men rose up from feast,
  And warm west wind grew east, and warm day night.

II

'Come snow, come wind or thunder
   High up in air,
I watch my face, and wonder
   At my bright hair;
Nought else exalts or grieves
The rose at heart, that heaves
   With love of her own leaves and lips that pair.

'She knows not loves that kissed her
   She knows not where.
Art thou the ghost, my sister,   30
   White sister there,
Am I the ghost, who knows?
My hand, a fallen rose,
   Lies snow-white on white snows, and takes no care.

'I cannot see what pleasures
   Or what pains were;
What pale new loves and treasures
   New years will bear;
What beam will fall, what shower,
What grief or joy for dower;   40
   But one thing knows the flower; the flower is fair.'

III

Glad, but not flushed with gladness,
   Since joys go by;
Sad, but not bent with sadness,
   Since sorrows die;
Deep in the gleaming glass
She sees all past things pass,
   And all sweet life that was lie down and lie.

There glowing ghosts of flowers
   Draw down, draw nigh;   50
And wings of swift spent hours
   Take flight and fly;
She sees by formless gleams,

She hears across cold streams,
    Dead mouths of many dreams that sing and sigh.

Face fallen and white throat lifted,
    With sleepless eye
She sees old loves that drifted,
    She knew not why,
Old loves and faded fears   60
Float down a stream that hears
    The flowing of all men's tears beneath the sky.

The Garden of Proserpine

Here, where the world is quiet;
    Here, where all trouble seems
Dead winds' and spent waves' riot
    In doubtful dreams of dreams;
I watch the green field growing
For reaping folk and sowing,
For harvest-time and mowing,
    A sleepy world of streams.

I am tired of tears and laughter,
    And men that laugh and weep;   10
Of what may come hereafter
    For men that sow to reap:
I am weary of days and hours,
Blown buds of barren flowers,
Desires and dreams and powers
    And everything but sleep.

Here life has death for neighbour,
    And far from eye or ear
Wan waves and wet winds labour,
    Weak ships and spirits steer;   20

They drive adrift, and whither
They wot not who make thither;
But no such winds blow hither,
   And no such things grow here.

No growth of moor or coppice,
   No heather-flower or vine,
But bloomless buds of poppies,
   Green grapes of Proserpine,
Pale beds of blowing rushes
Where no leaf blooms or blushes   30
Save this whereout she crushes
   For dead men deadly wine.

Pale, without name or number,
   In fruitless fields of corn,
They bow themselves and slumber
   All night till light is born;
And like a soul belated,
In hell and heaven unmated,
By cloud and mist abated
   Comes out of darkness morn.   40

Though one were strong as seven,
   He too with death shall dwell,
Nor wake with wings in heaven,
   Nor weep for pains in hell;
Though one were fair as roses,
His beauty clouds and closes;
And well though love reposes,
   In the end it is not well.

Pale, beyond porch and portal,
   Crowned with calm leaves, she stands   50
Who gathers all things mortal
   With cold immortal hands;
Her languid lips are sweeter
Than love's who fears to greet her
To men that mix and meet her
   From many times and lands.

She waits for each and other,
    She waits for all men born;
Forgets the earth her mother,
    The life of fruits and corn;
And spring and seed and swallow
Take wing for her and follow
Where summer song rings hollow
    And flowers are put to scorn.

There go the loves that wither,
    The old loves with wearier wings;
And all dead years draw thither,
    And all disastrous things;
Dead dreams of days forsaken,
Blind buds that snows have shaken,
Wild leaves that winds have taken,
    Red strays of ruined springs.

We are not sure of sorrow,
    And joy was never sure;
Today will die tomorrow;
    Time stoops to no man's lure;
And love, grown faint and fretful,
With lips but half regretful
Sighs, and with eyes forgetful
    Weeps that no loves endure.

From too much love of living,
    From hope and fear set free,
We thank with brief thanksgiving
    Whatever gods may be
That no life lives for ever;
That dead men rise up never;
That even the weariest river
    Winds somewhere safe to sea.

Then star nor sun shall waken,
    Nor any change of light:
Nor sound of waters shaken,

Nor any sound or sight:
Nor wintry leaves nor vernal,
Nor days nor things diurnal;
Only the sleep eternal
    In an eternal night.

The Sundew

A little marsh-plant, yellow green,
And pricked at lip with tender red.
Tread close, and either way you tread
Some faint black water jets between
Lest you should bruise the curious head.

A live thing maybe; who shall know?
The summer knows and suffers it;
For the cool moss is thick and sweet
Each side, and saves the blossom so
That it lives out the long June heat.   10

The deep scent of the heather burns
About it; breathless though it be,
Bow down and worship; more than we
Is the least flower whose life returns,
Least weed renascent in the sea.

We are vexed and cumbered in earth's sight
With wants, with many memories;
These see their mother what she is,
Glad-growing, till August leave more bright
The apple-coloured cranberries.   20

Wind blows and bleaches the strong grass,
Blown all one way to shelter it
From trample of strayed kine, with feet

Felt heavier than the moorhen was,
Strayed up past patches of wild wheat.

You call it sundew: how it grows,
If with its colour it have breath,
If life taste sweet to it, if death
Pain its soft petal, no man knows:
Man has no sight or sense that saith.   30

My sundew, grown of gentle days,
In these green miles the spring begun
Thy growth ere April had half done
With the soft secret of her ways
Or June made ready for the sun.

O red-lipped mouth of marsh-flower,
I have a secret halved with thee.
The name that is love's name to me
Thou knowest, and the face of her
Who is my festival to see.   40

The hard sun, as thy petals knew,
Coloured the heavy moss-water:
Thou wert not worth green midsummer
Nor fit to live to August blue,
O sundew, not remembering her.

Sapphics

All the night sleep came not upon my eyelids,
Shed not dew, nor shook nor unclosed a feather,
Yet with lips shut close and with eyes of iron
    Stood and beheld me.

Then to me so lying awake a vision
Came without sleep over the seas and touched me,

Softly touched mine eyelids and lips; and I too,
    Full of the vision,

Saw the white implacable Aphrodite,
Saw the hair unbound and the feet unsandalled   10
Shine as fire of sunset on western waters;
    Saw the reluctant

Feet, the straining plumes of the doves that drew her,
Looking always, looking with necks reverted,
Back to Lesbos, back to the hills whereunder
    Shone Mitylene;

Heard the flying feet of the Loves behind her
Make a sudden thunder upon the waters,
As the thunder flung from the strong unclosing
    Wings of a great wind.   20

So the goddess fled from her place, with awful
Sound of feet and thunder of wings around her;
While behind a clamour of singing women
    Severed the twilight.

Ah the singing, ah the delight, the passion!
All the Loves wept, listening; sick with anguish,
Stood the crowned nine Muses about Apollo;
    Fear was upon them,

While the tenth sang wonderful things they knew not.
Ah the tenth, the Lesbian! the nine were silent,   30
None endured the sound of her song for weeping;
    Laurel by laurel,

Faded all their crowns; but about her forehead,
Round her woven tresses and ashen temples
White as dead snow, paler than grass in summer,
    Ravaged with kisses,

Shone a light of fire as a crown for ever.
Yea, almost the implacable Aphrodite

Paused, and almost wept; such a song was that song.
  Yea, by her name too 40

Called her, saying, 'Turn to me, O my Sappho';
Yet she turned her face from the Loves, she saw not
Tears for laughter darken immortal eyelids,
  Heard not about her

Fearful fitful wings of the doves departing,
Saw not how the bosom of Aphrodite
Shook with weeping, saw not her shaken raiment,
  Saw not her hands wrung;

Saw the Lesbians kissing across their smitten
Lutes with lips more sweet than the sound of lute-strings, 50
Mouth to mouth and hand upon hand, her chosen,
  Fairer than all men;

Only saw the beautiful lips and fingers,
Full of songs and kisses and little whispers,
Full of music; only beheld among them
  Soar, as a bird soars

Newly fledged, her visible song, a marvel,
Made of perfect sound and exceeding passion,
Sweetly shapen, terrible, full of thunders,
  Clothed with the wind's wings. 60

Then rejoiced she, laughing with love, and scattered
Roses, awful roses of holy blossom;
Then the Loves thronged sadly with hidden faces
  Round Aphrodite,

Then the Muses, stricken at heart, were silent;
Yea, the gods waxed pale; such a song was that song.
All reluctant, all with a fresh repulsion,
  Fled from before her.

All withdrew long since, and the land was barren,
Full of fruitless women and music only. 70

Now perchance, when winds are assuaged at sunset,
  Lulled at the dewfall,

By the grey sea-side, unassuaged, unheard of,
Unbeloved, unseen in the ebb of twilight,
Ghosts of outcast women return lamenting,
  Purged not in Lethe,

Clothed about with flame and with tears, and singing
Songs that move the heart of the shaken heaven,
Songs that break the heart of the earth with pity,
  Hearing, to hear them.   80

August

There were four apples on the bough,
Half gold half red, that one might know
The blood was ripe inside the core;
The colour of the leaves was more
Like stems of yellow corn that grow
Through all the gold June meadow's floor.

The warm smell of the fruit was good
To feed on, and the split green wood,
With all its bearded lips and stains
Of mosses in the cloven veins,   10
Most pleasant, if one lay or stood
In sunshine or in happy rains.

There were four apples on the tree,
Red stained through gold, that all might see
The sun went warm from core to rind;
The green leaves made the summer blind
In that soft place they kept for me
With golden apples shut behind.

The leaves caught gold across the sun,
And where the bluest air begun   20
Thirsted for song to help the heat;
As I to feel my lady's feet
Draw close before the day were done;
Both lips grew dry with dreams of it.

In the mute August afternoon
They trembled to some undertune
Of music in the silver air;
Great pleasure was it to be there
Till green turned duskier and the moon
Coloured the corn-sheaves like gold hair.   30

That August time it was delight
To watch the red moons wane to white
'Twixt grey seamed stems of apple-trees;
A sense of heavy harmonies
Grew on the growth of patient night,
More sweet than shapen music is.

But some three hours before the moon
The air, still eager from the noon,
Flagged after heat, not wholly dead;
Against the stem I leant my head;   40
The colour soothed me like a tune,
Green leaves all round the gold and red.

I lay there till the warm smell grew
More sharp, when flecks of yellow dew
Between the round ripe leaves had blurred
The rind with stain and wet; I heard
A wind that blew and breathed and blew,
Too weak to alter its one word.

The wet leaves next the gentle fruit
Felt smoother, and the brown tree-root   50
Felt the mould warmer: I too felt
(As water feels the slow gold melt

Right through it when the day burns mute)
The peace of time wherein love dwelt.

There were four apples on the tree,
Gold stained on red that all might see
The sweet blood filled them to the core:
The colour of her hair is more
Like stems of fair faint gold, that be
Mown from the harvest's middle floor.   60

Hertha

I am that which began;
    Out of me the years roll;
Out of me God and man;
    I am equal and whole;
God changes, and man, and the form of them bodily;
    I am the soul.

Before ever land was,
    Before ever the sea,
Or soft hair of the grass,
    Or fair limbs of the tree,   10
Or the flesh-coloured fruit of my branches, I was,
    and thy soul was in me.

First life on my sources
    First drifted and swam;
Out of me are the forces
    That save it or damn;
Out of me man and woman, and wild-beast and bird;
    before God was, I am.

Beside or above me
    Nought is there to go;   20
Love or unlove me,
    Unknow me or know,

I am that which unloves me and loves; I am stricken,
    and I am the blow.

    I the mark that is missed
       And the arrows that miss,
    I the mouth that is kissed
       And the breath in the kiss,
The search, and the sought, and the seeker, the soul
    and the body that is.   30

    I am that thing which blesses
       My spirit elate;
    That which caresses
       With hands uncreate
My limbs unbegotten that measure the length of the
    measure of fate.

    But what thing dost thou now,
       Looking Godward, to cry
    'I am I, thou art thou,
       I am low, thou art high'?   40
I am thou, whom thou seekest to find him; find thou
    but thyself, thou art I.

    I the grain and the furrow,
       The plough-cloven clod
    And the ploughshare drawn thorough,
       The germ and the sod,
The deed and the doer, the seed and the sower, the
    dust which is God.

    Hast thou known how I fashioned thee,
       Child, underground?   50
    Fire that impassioned thee,
       Iron that bound,
Dim changes of water, what thing of all these hast
    thou known of or found?

    Canst thou say in thine heart
       Thou hast seen with thine eyes

With what cunning of art
    Thou wast wrought in what wise,
By what force of what stuff thou wast shapen, and
    shown on my breast to the skies?   60

Who hath given, who hath sold it thee,
    Knowledge of me?
Hath the wilderness told it thee?
    Hast thou learnt of the sea?
Hast thou communed in spirit with night? have the
    winds taken counsel with thee?

Have I set such a star
    To show light on thy brow
That thou sawest from afar
    What I show to thee now?   70
Have ye spoken as brethren together, the sun and
    the mountains and thou?

What is here, dost thou know it?
    What was, hast thou known?
Prophet nor poet
    Nor tripod nor throne
Nor spirit nor flesh can make answer, but only thy
    mother alone.

Mother, not maker,
    Born, and not made;   80
Though her children forsake her,
    Allured or afraid,
Praying prayers to the God of their fashion, she stirs
    not for all that have prayed.

A creed is a rod,
    And a crown is of night;
But this thing is God,
    To be man with thy might,
To grow straight in the strength of thy spirit, and
    live out thy life as the light.   90

I am in thee to save thee,
    As my soul in thee saith;
Give thou as I gave thee,
    Thy life-blood and breath,
Green leaves of thy labour, white flowers of thy
    thought, and red fruit of thy death.

Be the ways of thy giving
    As mine were to thee;
The free life of thy living,
    Be the gift of it free;   100
Not as servant to lord, nor as master to slave, shalt
    thou give thee to me.

O children of banishment,
    Souls overcast,
Were the lights ye see vanish meant
    Alway to last,
Ye would know not the sun overshining the shadows
    and stars overpast.

I that saw where ye trod
    The dim paths of the night   110
Set the shadow called God
    In your skies to give light;
But the morning of manhood is risen, and the shadowless
    soul is in sight.

The tree many-rooted
    That swells to the sky
With frondage red-fruited,
    The life-tree am I;
In the buds of your lives is the sap of my leaves: ye
    shall live and not die.   120

But the Gods of your fashion
    That take and that give,

In their pity and passion
That scourge and forgive,
They are worms that are bred in the bark that falls
off; they shall die and not live.

My own blood is what stanches
The wounds in my bark;
Stars caught in my branches
Make day of the dark,   130
And are worshipped as suns till the sunrise shall
tread out their fires as a spark.

Where dead ages hide under
The live roots of the tree,
In my darkness the thunder
Makes utterance of me;
In the clash of my boughs with each other ye hear
the waves sound of the sea.

That noise is of Time,
As his feathers are spread   140
And his feet set to climb
Through the boughs overhead,
And my foliage rings round him and rustles, and
branches are bent with his tread.

The storm-winds of ages
Blow through me and cease,
The war-wind that rages,
The spring-wind of peace,
Ere the breath of them roughen my tresses, ere one
of my blossoms increase.   150

All sounds of all changes,
All shadows and lights
On the world's mountain-ranges
And stream-riven heights,
Whose tongue is the wind's tongue and language of
storm-clouds on earth-shaking nights;

All forms of all faces,
   All works of all hands
In unsearchable places
   Of time-stricken lands,   160
All death and all life, and all reigns and all ruins,
   drop through me as sands.

   Though sore be my burden
     And more than ye know,
And my growth have no guerdon
     But only to grow,
Yet I fail not of growing for lightnings above me or
   deathworms below.

   These too have their part in me,
     As I too in these;   170
Such fire is at heart in me,
     Such sap is this tree's,
Which hath in it all sounds and all secrets of infinite
   lands and of seas.

   In the spring-coloured hours
     When my mind was as May's,
There brake forth of me flowers
     By centuries of days,
Strong blossoms with perfume of manhood, shot
   out from my spirit as rays.   180

   And the sound of them springing
     And smell of their shoots
Were as warmth and sweet singing
     And strength to my roots;
And the lives of my children made perfect with
   freedom of soul were my fruits.

   I bid you but be;
     I have need not of prayer;
I have need of you free
     As your mouths of mine air;   190

That my heart may be greater within me, beholding
   the fruits of me fair.

      More fair than strange fruit is
        Of faiths ye espouse;
      In me only the root is
        That blooms in your boughs;
Behold now your God that ye made you, to feed him
   with faith of your vows.

      In the darkening and whitening
        Abysses adored,   200
      With dayspring and lightning
        For lamp and for sword,
God thunders in heaven, and his angels were red with
   the wrath of the Lord.

      O my sons, O too dutiful
        Toward Gods not of me,
      Was not I enough beautiful?
        Was it hard to be free?
For behold, I am with you, am in you and of you;
   look forth now and see.   210

      Lo, winged with world's wonders,
        With miracles shod,
      With the fires of his thunders
        For raiment and rod,
God trembles in heaven, and his angels are white
   with the terror of God.

      For his twilight is come on him,
        His anguish is here;
      And his spirits gaze dumb on him,
        Grown grey from his fear;   220
And his hour taketh hold on him stricken, the last
   of his infinite year.

      Thought made him and breaks him,
        Truth slays and forgives;

But to you, as time takes him,
    This new thing it gives,
Even love, the beloved Republic, that feeds upon
    freedom and lives.

For truth only is living,
    Truth only is whole,   230
And the love of his giving
    Man's polestar and pole;
Man, pulse of my centre, and fruit of my body, and
    seed of my soul.

One birth of my bosom;
    One beam of mine eye;
One topmost blossom
    That scales the sky;
Man, equal and one with me, man that is made of
    me, man that is I.   240

Genesis

In the outer world that was before this earth,
    That was before all shape or space was born,
Before the blind first hour of time had birth,
    Before night knew the moonlight or the morn;

Yea, before any world had any light,
    Or anything called God or man drew breath,
Slowly the strong sides of the heaving night
    Moved, and brought forth the strength of life and death.

And the sad shapeless horror increate
    That was all things and one thing, without fruit,   10
Limit, or law; where love was none, nor hate,
    Where no leaf came to blossom from no root;

The very darkness that time knew not of,
    Nor God laid hand on, nor was man found there,
Ceased, and was cloven in several shapes; above
    Light, and night under, and fire, earth, water, and air.

Sunbeams and starbeams, and all coloured things,
    All forms and all similitudes began;
And death, the shadow cast by life's wide wings,
    And God, the shade cast by the soul of man.   20

Then between shadow and substance, night and light,
    Then between birth and death, and deeds and days,
The illimitable embrace and the amorous fight
    That of itself begets, bears, rears, and slays,

The immortal war of mortal things, that is
    Labour and life and growth and good and ill,
The mild antiphonies that melt and kiss,
    The violent symphonies that meet and kill,

All nature of all things began to be.
    But chiefliest in the spirit (beast or man,   30
Planet of heaven or blossom of earth or sea)
    The divine contraries of life began.

For the great labour of growth, being many, is one;
    One thing the white death and the ruddy birth;
The invisible air and the all-beholden sun,
    And barren water and many-childed earth.

And these things are made manifest in men
    From the beginning forth unto this day:
Time writes and life records them, and again
    Death seals them lest the record pass away.   40

For if death were not, then should growth not be,
    Change, nor the life of good nor evil things;
Nor were there night at all nor light to see,
    Nor water of sweet nor water of bitter springs.

For in each man and each year that is born
    Are sown the twin seeds of the strong twin powers;
The white seed of the fruitful helpful morn,
    The black seed of the barren hurtful hours.

And he that of the black seed eateth fruit,
    To him the savour as honey shall be sweet;   50
And he in whom the white seed hath struck root,
    He shall have sorrow and trouble and tears for meat.

And him whose lips the sweet fruit hath made red
    In the end men loathe and make his name a rod;
And him whose mouth on the unsweet fruit hath fed
    In the end men follow and know for very God.

And of these twain, the black seed and the white,
    All things come forth, endured of men and done;
And still the day is great with child of night,
    And still the black night labours with the sun.   60

And each man and each year that lives on earth
    Turns hither or thither, and hence or thence is fed;
And as a man before was from his birth,
    So shall a man be after among the dead.

Cor Cordium

    O heart of hearts, the chalice of love's fire,
        Hid round with flowers and all the bounty of bloom;
        O wonderful and perfect heart, for whom
    The lyrist liberty made life a lyre;
    O heavenly heart, at whose most dear desire
        Dead love, living and singing, cleft his tomb,
        And with him risen and regent in death's room

All day thy choral pulses rang full choir;
O heart whose beating blood was running song,
   O sole thing sweeter than thine own songs were,
    Help us for thy free love's sake to be free,
True for thy truth's sake, for thy strength's sake strong,
   Till very liberty make clean and fair
    The nursing earth as the sepulchral sea.

A Forsaken Garden

In a coign of the cliff between lowland and highland,
   At the sea-down's edge between windward and lee,
Walled round with rocks as an inland island,
   The ghost of a garden fronts the sea.
A girdle of brushwood and thorn encloses
   The steep square slope of the blossomless bed
Where the weeds that grew green from the graves of its roses
    Now lie dead.

The fields fall southward, abrupt and broken,
   To the low last edge of the long lone land.   10
If a step should sound or a word be spoken,
   Would a ghost not rise at the strange guest's hand?
So long have the grey bare walks lain guestless,
   Through branches and briars if a man make way,
He shall find no life but the sea-wind's, restless
    Night and day.

The dense hard passage is blind and stifled
   That crawls by a track none turn to climb
To the strait waste place that the years have rifled
   Of all but the thorns that are touched not of time.   20
The thorns he spares when the rose is taken;
   The rocks are left when he wastes the plain.
The wind that wanders, the weeds wind-shaken,
    These remain.

Not a flower to be pressed of the foot that falls not;
    As the heart of a dead man the seed-plots are dry;
From the thicket of thorns whence the nightingale calls not,
    Could she call, there were never a rose to reply.
Over the meadows that blossom and wither
    Rings but the note of a sea-bird's song;
Only the sun and the rain come hither
        All year long.   30

The sun burns sere and the rain dishevels
    One gaunt bleak blossom of scentless breath.
Only the wind here hovers and revels
    In a round where life seems barren as death.
Here there was laughing of old, there was weeping,
    Haply, of lovers none ever will know,
Whose eyes went seaward a hundred sleeping
        Years ago.   40

Heart handfast in heart as they stood, 'Look thither',
    Did he whisper? 'look forth from the flowers to the sea;
For the foam-flowers endure when the rose-blossoms wither,
    And men that love lightly may die – but we?'
And the same wind sang and the same waves whitened,
    And or ever the garden's last petals were shed,
In the lips that had whispered, the eyes that had lightened,
        Love was dead.

Or they loved their life through, and then went whither?
    And were one to the end – but what end who knows?   50
Love deep as the sea as a rose must wither,
    As the rose-red seaweed that mocks the rose.
Shall the dead take thought for the dead to love them?
    What love was ever as deep as a grave?
They are loveless now as the grass above them
        Or the wave.

All are at one now, roses and lovers,
    Not known of the cliffs and the fields and the sea.
Not a breath of the time that has been hovers
    In the air now soft with a summer to be.   60

Not a breath shall there sweeten the seasons hereafter
    Of the flowers or the lovers that laugh now or weep,
When as they that are free now of weeping and laughter
        We shall sleep.

Here death may deal not again for ever;
    Here change may come not till all change end.
From the graves they have made they shall rise up never,
    Who have left nought living to ravage and rend.
Earth, stones, and thorns of the wild ground growing,
    While the sun and the rain live, these shall be;   70
Till a last wind's breath upon all these blowing
        Roll the sea.

Till the slow sea rise and the sheer cliff crumble,
    Till terrace and meadow the deep gulfs drink,
Till the strength of the waves of the high tides humble
    The fields that lessen, the rocks that shrink,
Here now in his triumph where all things falter,
    Stretched out on the spoils that his own hand spread,
As a god self-slain on his own strange altar,
        Death lies dead.   80

Relics

This flower that smells of honey and the sea,
White laurustine, seems in my hand to be
    A white star made of memory long ago
Lit in the heaven of dear times dead to me.

A star out of the skies love used to know
Here held in hand, a stray left yet to show
    What flowers my heart was full of in the days
That are long since gone down dead memory's flow.

Dead memory that revives on doubtful ways,
Half hearkening what the buried season says   10

Out of the world of the unapparent dead
Where the lost Aprils are, and the lost Mays.

Flower, once I knew thy star-white brethren bred
Nigh where the last of all the land made head
   Against the sea, a keen-faced promontory,
Flowers on salt wind and sprinkled sea-dews fed.

Their hearts were glad of the free place's glory;
The wind that sang them all his stormy story
   Had talked all winter to the sleepless spray,
And as the sea's their hues were hard and hoary.   20

Like things born of the sea and the bright day,
They laughed out at the years that could not slay,
   Live sons and joyous of unquiet hours,
And stronger than all storms that range for prey.

And in the close indomitable flowers
A keen-edged odour of the sun and showers
   Was as the smell of the fresh honeycomb
Made sweet for mouths of none but paramours.

Out of the hard green wall of leaves that clomb
They showed like windfalls of the snow-soft foam,   30
   Or feathers from the weary south-wind's wing,
Fair as the spray that it came shoreward from.

And thou, as white, what word hast thou to bring?
If my heart hearken, whereof wilt thou sing?
   For some sign surely thou too hast to bear,
Some word far south was taught thee of the spring.

White like a white rose, not like these that were
Taught of the wind's mouth and the winter air,
   Poor tender thing of soft Italian bloom,
Where once thou grewest, what else for me grew there?   40

Born in what spring and on what city's tomb,
By whose hand wast thou reached, and plucked for whom?

    There hangs about thee, could the soul's sense tell,
An odour as of love and of love's doom.

Of days more sweet than thou wast sweet to smell,
Of flower-soft thoughts that came to flower and fell,
    Of loves that lived a lily's life and died,
Of dreams now dwelling where dead roses dwell.

O white birth of the golden mountain-side
That for the sun's love makes its bosom wide   50
    At sunrise, and with all its woods and flowers
Takes in the morning to its heart of pride!

Thou hast a word of that one land of ours,
And of the fair town called of the Fair Towers,
    A word for me of my San Gimignan,
A word of April's greenest-girdled hours.

Of the old breached walls whereon the wallflowers ran
Called of Saint Fina, breachless now of man,
    Though time with soft feet break them stone by stone,
Who breaks down hour by hour his own reign's span.   60

Of the old cliff overcome and overgrown
That all that flowerage clothed as flesh clothes bone,
    That garment of acacias made for May,
Whereof here lies one witness overblown.

The fair brave trees with all their flowers at play,
How king-like they stood up into the day!
    How sweet the day was with them, and the night!
Such words of message have dead flowers to say.

This that the winter and the wind made bright,
And this that lived upon Italian light,   70
    Before I throw them and these words away,
Who knows but I what memories too take flight?

A Ballad of Dreamland

I hid my heart in a nest of roses,
    Out of the sun's way, hidden apart;
In a softer bed than the soft white snow's is,
    Under the roses I hid my heart.
    Why would it sleep not? why should it start,
When never a leaf of the rose-tree stirred?
    What made sleep flutter his wings and part?
Only the song of a secret bird.

Lie still, I said, for the wind's wing closes,
    And mild leaves muffle the keen sun's dart;   10
Lie still, for the wind on the warm sea dozes,
    And the wind is unquieter yet than thou art.
    Does a thought in thee still as a thorn's wound smart?
Does the fang still fret thee of hope deferred?
    What bids the lids of thy sleep dispart?
Only the song of a secret bird.

The green land's name that a charm encloses,
    It never was writ in the traveller's chart,
And sweet on its trees as the fruit that grows is,
    It never was sold in the merchant's mart.   20
    The swallows of dreams through its dim fields dart,
And sleep's are the tunes in its tree-tops heard;
    No hound's note wakens the wildwood hart,
Only the song of a secret bird.

ENVOI

In the world of dreams I have chosen my part,
    To sleep for a season and hear no word
Of true love's truth or of light love's art,
    Only the song of a secret bird.

A Vision of Spring in Winter

I

O tender time that love thinks long to see,
    Sweet foot of spring that with her footfall sows
    Late snowlike flowery leavings of the snows,
Be not too long irresolute to be;
O mother-month, where have they hidden thee?
    Out of the pale time of the flowerless rose
I reach my heart out toward the springtime lands,
    I stretch my spirit forth to the fair hours,
        The purplest of the prime;
I lean my soul down over them, with hands   10
    Made wide to take the ghostly growths of flowers;
        I send my love back to the lovely time.

II

Where has the greenwood hid thy gracious head?
    Veiled with what visions while the grey world grieves,
    Or muffled with what shadows of green leaves,
What warm intangible green shadows spread
To sweeten the sweet twilight for thy bed?
    What sleep enchants thee? what delight deceives?
Where the deep dreamlike dew before the dawn
    Feels not the fingers of the sunlight yet   20
        Its silver web unweave,
Thy footless ghost on some unfooted lawn
    Whose air the unrisen sunbeams fear to fret
        Lives a ghost's life of daylong dawn and eve.

III

Sunrise it sees not, neither set of star,
    Large nightfall, nor imperial plenilune,
    Nor strong sweet shape of the full-breasted noon;
But where the silver-sandalled shadows are,
Too soft for arrows of the sun to mar,
    Moves with the mild gait of an ungrown moon: 30
Hard overhead the half-lit crescent swims,
    The tender-coloured night draws hardly breath,

The light is listening;
They watch the dawn of slender-shapen limbs,
    Virginal, born again of doubtful death,
        Chill foster-father of the weanling spring.

                              IV

As sweet desire of day before the day,
    As dreams of love before the true love born,
    From the outer edge of winter overworn
The ghost arisen of May before the May   40
Takes through dim air her unawakened way,
    The gracious ghost of morning risen ere morn.
With little unblown breasts and child-eyed looks
    Following, the very maid, the girl-child spring,
        Lifts windward her bright brows,
Dips her light feet in warm and moving brooks,
    And kindles with her own mouth's colouring
        The fearful firstlings of the plumeless boughs.

                              V

I seek thee sleeping, and awhile I see,
    Fair face that art not, how thy maiden breath   50
    Shall put at last the deadly days to death
And fill the fields and fire the woods with thee
And seaward hollows where my feet would be
    When heaven shall hear the word that April saith
To change the cold heart of the weary time,
    To stir and soften all the time to tears,
        Tears joyfuller than mirth;
As even to May's clear height the young days climb
    With feet not swifter than those fair first years
        Whose flowers revive not with thy flowers on earth.   60

                              VI

I would not bid thee, though I might, give back
    One good thing youth has given and borne away;
    I crave not any comfort of the day
That is not, nor on time's retrodden track
Would turn to meet the white-robed hours or black
    That long since left me on their mortal way;

Nor light nor love that has been, nor the breath
   That comes with morning from the sun to be
      And sets light hope on fire;
No fruit, no flower thought once too fair for death,   70
   No flower nor hour once fallen from life's green tree,
      No leaf once plucked or once fulfilled desire.

VII

The morning song beneath the stars that fled
   With twilight through the moonless mountain air,
   While youth with burning lips and wreathless hair
Sang toward the sun that was to crown his head,
Rising; the hopes that triumphed and fell dead,
   The sweet swift eyes and songs of hours that were;
These may'st thou not give back for ever; these,
   As at the sea's heart all her wrecks lie waste,   80
      Lie deeper than the sea;
But flowers thou may'st, and winds, and hours of ease,
   And all its April to the world thou may'st
      Give back, and half my April back to me.

On the Cliffs

ἱμερόφωνος ἀηδών.
SAPPHO

Between the moondawn and the sundown here
The twilight hangs half starless; half the sea
Still quivers as for love or pain or fear
Or pleasure mightier than these all may be
A man's live heart might beat
Wherein a God's with mortal blood should meet
And fill its pulse too full to bear the strain
With fear or love or pleasure's twin-born, pain.
Fiercely the gaunt woods to the grim soil cling
That bears for all fair fruits   10
Wan wild sparse flowers of windy and wintry spring

Between the tortive serpent-shapen roots
Wherethrough their dim growth hardly strikes and shoots
And shews one gracious thing
Hardly, to speak for summer one sweet word
Of summer's self scarce heard.
But higher the steep green sterile fields, thick-set
With flowerless hawthorn even to the upward verge
Whence the woods gathering watch new cliffs emerge
Higher than their highest of crowns that sea-winds fret,   20
Hold fast, for all that night or wind can say,
Some pale pure colour yet,
Too dim for green and luminous for grey.
Between the climbing inland cliffs above
And these beneath that breast and break the bay,
A barren peace too soft for hate or love
Broods on an hour too dim for night or day.

O wind, O wingless wind that walk'st the sea,
Weak wind, wing-broken, wearier wind than we,
Who are yet not spirit-broken, maimed like thee,   30
Who wail not in our inward night as thou
In the outer darkness now,
What word has the old sea given thee for mine ear
From thy faint lips to hear?
For some word would she send me, knowing not how.

Nay, what far other word
Than ever of her was spoken, or of me
Or all my winged white kinsfolk of the sea
Between fresh wave and wave was ever heard,
Cleaves the clear dark enwinding tree with tree   40
Too close for stars to separate and to see
Enmeshed in multitudinous unity?
What voice of what strong God hath stormed and stirred
The fortressed rock of silence, rent apart
Even to the core Night's all-maternal heart?
What voice of God grown heavenlier in a bird,
Made keener of edge to smite
Than lightning – yea, thou knowest, O mother Night,
Keen as that cry from thy strange children sent

Wherewith the Athenian judgment-shrine was rent,   50
For wrath that all their wrath was vainly spent,
Their wrath for wrong made right
By justice in her own divine despite
That bade pass forth unblamed
The sinless matricide and unashamed?
Yea, what new cry is this, what note more bright
Than their song's wing of words was dark of flight,
What word is this thou hast heard,
Thine and not thine or theirs, O Night, what word
More keen than lightning and more sweet than light?   60
As all men's hearts grew godlike in one bird
And all those hearts cried on thee, crying with might,
Hear us, O mother Night.

Dumb is the mouth of darkness as of death:
Light, sound and life are one
In the eyes and lips of dawn that draw the sun
To hear what first child's word with glimmering breath
Their weak wan weanling child the twilight saith;
But night makes answer none.

God, if thou be God, – bird, if bird thou be, –   70
Do thou then answer me.
For but one word, what wind soever blow,
Is blown up usward ever from the sea.
In fruitless years of youth dead long ago
And deep beneath their own dead leaves and snow
Buried, I heard with bitter heart and sere
The same sea's word unchangeable, nor knew
But that mine own life-days were changeless too
And sharp and salt with unshed tear on tear
And cold and fierce and barren; and my soul,   80
Sickening, swam weakly with bated breath
In a deep sea like death,
And felt the wind buffet her face with brine
Hard, and harsh thought on thought in long bleak roll
Blown by keen gusts of memory sad as thine
Heap the weight up of pain, and break, and leave
Strength scarce enough to grieve

In the sick heavy spirit, unmanned with strife
Of waves that beat at the tired lips of life.

Nay, sad may be man's memory, sad may be   90
The dream he weaves him as for shadow of thee,
But scarce one breathing-space, one heartbeat long,
Wilt thou take shadow of sadness on thy song.
Not thou, being more than man or man's desire,
Being bird and God in one,
With throat of gold and spirit of the sun;
The sun whom all our souls and songs call sire,
Whose godhead gave thee, chosen of all our quire,
Thee only of all that serve, of all that sing
Before our sire and king,
Borne up some space on time's world-wandering wing,   100
This gift, this doom, to bear till time's wing tire –
Life everlasting of eternal fire.

Thee only of all; yet can no memory say
How many a night and day
My heart has been as thy heart, and my life
As thy life is, a sleepless hidden thing,
Full of the thirst and hunger of winter and spring,
That seeks its food not in such love or strife
As fill men's hearts with passionate hours and rest.   110
From no loved lips and on no loving breast
Have I sought ever for such gifts as bring
Comfort, to stay the secret soul with sleep.
The joys, the loves, the labours, whence men reap
Rathe fruit of hopes and fears,
I have made not mine; the best of all my days
Have been as those fair fruitless summer strays,
Those water-waifs that but the sea-wind steers,
Flakes of glad foam or flowers on footless ways
That take the wind in season and the sun,
And when the wind wills is their season done.   120

For all my days as all thy days from birth
My heart as thy heart was in me as thee,

Fire; and not all the fountains of the sea
Have waves enough to quench it, nor on earth
Is fuel enough to feed,
While day sows night and night sows day for seed.

We were not marked for sorrow, thou nor I,
For joy nor sorrow, sister, were we made,
To take delight and grief to live and die,   130
Assuaged by pleasures or by pains affrayed
That melt men's hearts and alter; we retain
A memory mastering pleasure and all pain,
A spirit within the sense of ear and eye,
A soul behind the soul, that seeks and sings
And makes our life move only with its wings
And feed but from its lips, that in return
Feed of our hearts wherein the old fires that burn
Have strength not to consume
Nor glory enough to exalt us past our doom.   140

Ah, ah, the doom (thou knowest whence rang that wail)
Of the shrill nightingale!
(From whose wild lips, thou knowest, that wail was thrown)
For round about her have the great gods cast
A wing-borne body, and clothed her close and fast
With a sweet life that hath no part in moan.
But me, for me (how hadst thou heart to hear?)
Remains a sundering with the two-edged spear.

Ah, for her doom! so cried in presage then
The bodeful bondslave of the king of men,   150
And might not win her will.
Too close the entangling dragnet woven of crime,
The snare of ill new-born of elder ill,
The curse of new time for an elder time,
Had caught, and held her yet,
Enmeshed intolerably in the intolerant net,
Who thought with craft to mock the God most high,
And win by wiles his crown of prophecy
From the Sun's hand sublime,
As God were man, to spare or to forget.   160

But thou, – the gods have given thee and forgiven thee
More than our master gave
That strange-eyed spirit-wounded strange-tongued slave
There questing houndlike where the roofs red-wet
Reeked as a wet red grave.
Life everlasting has their strange grace given thee,
Even hers whom thou wast wont to sing and serve
With eyes, but not with song, too swift to swerve;
Yet might not even thine eyes estranged estrange her,
Who seeing thee too, but inly, burn and bleed   170
Like that pale princess-priest of Priam's seed,
For stranger service gave thee guerdon stranger;
If this indeed be guerdon, this indeed
Her mercy, this thy meed –
That thou, being more than all we born, being higher
Than all heads crowned of him that only gives
The light whereby man lives,
The bay that bids man moved of God's desire
Lay hand on lute or lyre,
Set lip to trumpet or deflowered green reed –   180
If this were given thee for a grace indeed,
That thou, being first of all these, thou alone
Shouldst have the grace to die not, but to live
And lose nor change one pulse of song, one tone
Of all that were thy lady's and thine own,
Thy lady's whom thou criedst on to forgive,
Thou, priest and sacrifice on the altar-stone
Where none may worship not of all that live,
Love's priestess, errant on dark ways diverse;
If this were grace indeed for Love to give,   190
If this indeed were blessing and no curse.

Love's priestess, mad with pain and joy of song,
Song's priestess, mad with joy and pain of love,
Name above all names that are lights above,
We have loved, praised, pitied, crowned and done thee wrong,
O thou past praise and pity; thou the sole
Utterly deathless, perfect only and whole

Immortal, body and soul.
For over all whom time hath overpast
The shadow of sleep inexorable is cast,   200
The implacable sweet shadow of perfect sleep
That gives not back what life gives death to keep;
Yea, all that lived and loved and sang and sinned
Are all borne down death's cold sweet soundless wind
That blows all night and knows not whom its breath,
Darkling, may touch to death:
But one that wind hath touched and changed not, – one
Whose body and soul are parcel of the sun;
One that earth's fire could burn not, nor the sea
Quench; nor might human doom take hold on thee;   210
All praise, all pity, all dreams have done thee wrong,
All love, with eyes love-blinded from above;
Song's priestess, mad with joy and pain of love,
Love's priestess, mad with pain and joy of song.

Hast thou none other answer then for me
Than the air may have of thee,
Or the earth's warm woodlands girdling with green girth
Thy secret sleepless burning life on earth,
Or even the sea that once, being woman crowned
And girt with fire and glory of anguish round,   220
Thou wert so fain to seek to, fain to crave
If she would hear thee and save
And give thee comfort of thy great green grave?
Because I have known thee always who thou art,
Thou knowest, have known thee to thy heart's own heart,
Nor ever have given light ear to storied song
That did thy sweet name sweet unwitting wrong,
Nor ever have called thee nor would call for shame,
Thou knowest, but inly by thine only name,
Sappho – because I have known thee and loved, hast thou   230
None other answer now?
As brother and sister were we, child and bird,
Since thy first Lesbian word
Flamed on me, and I knew not whence I knew

This was the song that struck my whole soul through,
Pierced my keen spirit of sense with edge more keen,
Even when I knew not, – even ere sooth was seen, –
When thou wast but the tawny sweet winged thing
Whose cry was but of spring.

And yet even so thine ear should hear me – yea,   240
Hear me this nightfall by this northland bay,
Even for their sake whose loud good word I had,
Singing of thee in the all-beloved clime
Once, where the windy wine of spring makes mad
Our sisters of Majano, who kept time
Clear to my choral rhyme.
Yet was the song acclaimed of these aloud
Whose praise had made mute humbleness misproud,
The song with answering song applauded thus,
But of that Daulian dream of Itylus.   250
So but for love's love haply was it – nay,
How else? – that even their song took my song's part,
For love of love and sweetness of sweet heart,
Or god-given glorious madness of mid May
And heat of heart and hunger and thirst to sing,
Full of the new wine of the wind of spring.

Or if this were not, and it be not sin
To hold myself in spirit of thy sweet kin,
In heart and spirit of song;
If this my great love do thy grace no wrong,   260
Thy grace that gave me grace to dwell therein;
If thy gods thus be my gods, and their will
Made my song part of thy song – even such part
As man's hath of God's heart –
And my life like as thy life to fulfil;
What have our gods then given us? Ah, to thee,
Sister, much more, much happier than to me,
Much happier things they have given, and more of grace
Than falls to man's light race;
For lighter are we, all our love and pain   270
Lighter than thine, who knowest of time or place

Thus much, that place nor time
Can heal or hurt or lull or change again
The singing soul that makes his soul sublime
Who hears the far fall of its fire-fledged rhyme
Fill darkness as with bright and burning rain
Till all the live gloom inly glows, and light
Seems with the sound to cleave the core of night.

The singing soul that moves thee, and that moved
When thou wast woman, and their songs divine   280
Who mixed for Grecian mouths heaven's lyric wine
Fell dumb, fell down reproved
Before one sovereign Lesbian song of thine.
That soul, though love and life had fain held fast,
Wind-winged with fiery music, rose and past
Through the indrawn hollow of earth and heaven and hell,
As through some strait sea-shell
The wide sea's immemorial song, – the sea
That sings and breathes in strange men's ears of thee
How in her barren bride-bed, void and vast,   290
Even thy soul sang itself to sleep at last.

To sleep? Ah, then, what song is this, that here
Makes all the night one ear,
One ear fulfilled and mad with music, one
Heart kindling as the heart of heaven, to hear
A song more fiery than the awakening sun
Sings, when his song sets fire
To the air and clouds that build the dead night's pyre?
O thou of divers-coloured mind, O thou
Deathless, God's daughter subtle-souled – lo, now,   300
Now too the song above all songs, in flight
Higher than the day-star's height,
And sweet as sound the moving wings of night!
Thou of the divers-coloured seat – behold,
Her very song of old! –
O deathless, O God's daughter subtle-souled!
That same cry through this boskage overhead
Rings round reiterated,

Palpitates as the last palpitated,
The last that panted through her lips and died   310
Not down this grey north sea's half sapped cliff-side
That crumbles toward the coastline, year by year
More near the sands and near;
The last loud lyric fiery cry she cried,
Heard once on heights Leucadian, – heard not here.

Not here; for this that fires our northland night,
This is the song that made
Love fearful, even the heart of love afraid,
With the great anguish of its great delight.
No swan-song, no far-fluttering half-drawn breath,   320
No word that love of love's sweet nature saith,
No dirge that lulls the narrowing lids of death,
No healing hymn of peace-prevented strife, –
This is her song of life.

I loved thee, – hark, one tenderer note than all –
Atthis, of old time, once – one low long fall,
Sighing – one long low lovely loveless call,
Dying – one pause in song so flamelike fast –
Atthis, long since in old time overpast –
One soft first pause and last.   330
One, – then the old rage of rapture's fieriest rain
Storms all the music-maddened night again.

Child of God, close craftswoman, I beseech thee,
Bid not ache nor agony break nor master,
Lady, my spirit –
O thou her mistress, might her cry not reach thee?
Our Lady of all men's loves, could Love go past her,
Pass, and not hear it?

She hears not as she heard not; hears not me,
O treble-natured mystery, – how should she   340
Hear, or give ear? – who heard and heard not thee;
Heard, and went past, and heard not; but all time
Hears all that all the ravin of his years

Hath cast not wholly out of all men's ears
And dulled to death with deep dense funeral chime
Of their reiterate rhyme.
And now of all songs uttering all her praise,
All hers who had thy praise and did thee wrong,
Abides one song yet of her lyric days,
Thine only, this thy song.   350

O soul triune, woman and god and bird,
Man, man at least has heard.
All ages call thee conqueror, and thy cry
The mightiest as the least beneath the sky
Whose heart was ever set to song, or stirred
With wind of mounting music blown more high
Than wildest wing may fly,
Hath heard or hears, – even Æschylus as I.
But when thy name was woman, and thy word
Human, – then haply, surely then meseems   360
This thy bird's note was heard on earth of none,
Of none save only in dreams.
In all the world then surely was but one
Song; as in heaven at highest one sceptred sun
Regent, on earth here surely without fail
One only, one imperious nightingale.
Dumb was the field, the woodland mute, the lawn
Silent; the hill was tongueless as the vale
Even when the last fair waif of cloud that felt
Its heart beneath the colouring moonrays melt,   370
At high midnoon of midnight half withdrawn,
Bared all the sudden deep divine moondawn.
Then, unsaluted by her twin-born tune,
That latter timeless morning of the moon
Rose past its hour of moonrise; clouds gave way
To the old reconquering ray,
But no song answering made it more than day;
No cry of song by night
Shot fire into the cloud-constraining light.
One only, one Æolian island heard   380
Thrill, but through no bird's throat,

In one strange manlike maiden's godlike note,
The song of all these as a single bird.
Till the sea's portal was as funeral gate
For that sole singer in all time's ageless date
Singled and signed for so triumphal fate,
All nightingales but one in all the world
All her sweet life were silent; only then,
When her life's wing of womanhood was furled,
Their cry, this cry of thine was heard again,　　390
As of me now, of any born of men.

Through sleepless clear spring nights filled full of thee,
Rekindled here, thy ruling song has thrilled
The deep dark air and subtle tender sea
And breathless hearts with one bright sound fulfilled.
Or at midnoon to me
Swimming, and birds about my happier head
Skimming, one smooth soft way by water and air,
To these my bright born brethren and to me
Hath not the clear wind borne or seemed to bear　　400
A song wherein all earth and heaven and sea
Were molten in one music made of thee
To enforce us, O our sister of the shore,
Look once in heart back landward and adore?
For songless were we sea-mews, yet had we
More joy than all things joyful of thee – more,
Haply, than all things happiest; nay, save thee,
In thy strong rapture of imperious joy
Too high for heart of sea-borne bird or boy,
What living things were happiest if not we?　　410
But knowing not love nor change nor wrath nor wrong,
No more we knew of song.

Song, and the secrets of it, and their might,
What blessings curse it and what curses bless,
I know them since my spirit had first in sight,
Clear as thy song's words or the live sun's light,
The small dark body's Lesbian loveliness
That held the fire eternal; eye and ear

Were as a god's to see, a god's to hear,
Through all his hours of daily and nightly chime,   420
The sundering of the two-edged spear of time:
The spear that pierces even the sevenfold shields
Of mightiest Memory, mother of all songs made,
And wastes all songs as roseleaves kissed and frayed
As here the harvest of the foam-flowered fields;
But thine the spear may waste not that he wields
Since first the God whose soul is man's live breath,
The sun whose face hath our sun's face for shade,
Put all the light of life and love and death
Too strong for life, but not for love too strong,   430
Where pain makes peace with pleasure in thy song,
And in thine heart, where love and song make strife,
Fire everlasting of eternal life.

From **The Queen's Pleasance**

                    So they lay   362
Tranced once, nor watched along the fiery bay
The shine of summer darkness palpitate and play.
She had nor sight nor voice; her swooning eyes
Knew not if night or light were in the skies;
Across her beauty sheer the moondawn shed
Its light as on a thing as white and dead;
Only with stress of soft fierce hands she prest
Between the throbbing blossoms of her breast   370
His ardent face, and through his hair her breath
Went quivering as when life is hard on death;
And with strong trembling fingers she strained fast
His head into her bosom; till at last,
Satiate with sweetness of that burning bed,
His eyes afire with tears, he raised his head
And laughed into her lips; and all his heart
Filled hers; then face from face fell, and apart

Each hung on each with panting lips, and felt
Sense into sense and spirit in spirit melt.   380
   'Hast thou no sword? I would not live till day;
O love, this night and we must pass away,
It must die soon, and let not us die late.'
   'Take then my sword and slay me; nay, but wait
Till day be risen; what, wouldst thou think to die
Before the light take hold upon the sky?'
   'Yea, love; for how shall we have twice, being twain,
This very night of love's most rapturous reign?
Live thou and have thy day, and year by year
Be great, but what shall I be? Slay me here;   390
Let me die not when love lies dead, but now
Strike through my heart: nay, sweet, what heart hast thou?
Is it so much I ask thee, and spend my breath
In asking? nay, thou knowest it is but death.
Hadst thou true heart to love me, thou wouldst give
This: but for hate's sake thou wilt let me live.'
  Here he caught up her lips with his, and made
The wild prayer silent in her heart that prayed,
And strained her to him till all her faint breath sank
And her bright light limbs palpitated and shrank   400
And rose and fluctuated as flowers in rain
That bends them and they tremble and rise again
And heave and straighten and quiver all through with bliss
And turn afresh their mouths up for a kiss,
Amorous, athirst of that sweet influent love;
So, hungering towards his hovering lips above,
Her red-rose mouth yearned silent, and her eyes
Closed, and flashed after, as through June's darkest skies
The divine heartbeats of the deep live light
Make open and shut the gates of the outer night.   410
   Long lay they still, subdued with love, nor knew
If cloud or light changed colour as it grew,
If star or moon beheld them; if above
The heaven of night waxed fiery with their love,
Or earth beneath were moved at heart and root
To burn as they, to burn and bring forth fruit
Unseasonable for love's sake; if tall trees

Bowed, and close flowers yearned open, and the breeze
Failed and fell silent as a flame that fails:
And all that hour unheard the nightingales   420
Clamoured, and all the woodland soul was stirred,
And depth and height were one great song unheard,
As though the world caught music and took fire
From the instant heart alone of their desire.

The Lute and the Lyre

Deep desire, that pierces heart and spirit to the root,
Finds reluctant voice in verse that yearns like soaring fire,
Takes exultant voice when music holds in high pursuit
　　Deep desire.

Keen as burns the passion of the rose whose buds respire,
Strong as grows the yearning of the blossom toward the fruit,
Sounds the secret half unspoken ere the deep tones tire.

Slow subsides the rapture that possessed love's flower-soft lute,
Slow the palpitation of the triumph of the lyre:
Still the soul feels burn, a flame unslaked though these be mute,
　　Deep desire.

Plus Intra

Soul within sense, immeasurable, obscure,
Insepulchred and deathless, through the dense
Deep elements may scarce be felt as pure
　　Soul within sense.

From depth and height by measurers left immense,
Through sound and shape and colour, comes the
    unsure
Vague utterance, fitful with supreme suspense.

All that may pass, and all that must ensure,
Song speaks not, painting shows not: more intense
And keen than these, art wakes with music's lure
      Soul within sense.

The Roundel

A roundel is wrought as a ring or a starbright sphere,
With craft of delight and with cunning of sound unsought,
That the heart of the hearer may smile if to pleasure his ear
      A roundel is wrought.

Its jewel of music is carven of all or of aught –
Love, laughter, or mourning – remembrance of rapture or
    fear –
That fancy may fashion to hang in the ear of thought.

As a bird's quick song runs round, and the hearts in us hear
Pause answer to pause, and again the same strain caught,
So moves the device whence, round as a pearl or tear,
      A roundel is wrought.

Three Faces

I
VENTIMIGLIA
The sky and sea glared hard and bright and blank:
Down the one steep street, with slow steps firm and free,
A tall girl paced, with eyes too proud to thank
      The sky and sea.

One dead flat sapphire, void of wrath or glee,
Through bay on bay shone blind from bank to bank
The weary Mediterranean, drear to see.

More deep, more living, shone her eyes that drank
The breathless light and shed again on me,
Till pale before their splendour waned and shrank   10
    The sky and sea.

II
GENOA

Again the same strange might of eyes, that saw
In heaven and earth nought fairer, overcame
My sight with rapture of reiterate awe,
    Again the same.

The self-same pulse of wonder shook like flame
The spirit of sense within me: what strange law
Had bid this be, for blessing or for blame?

To what veiled end that fate or chance foresaw
Came forth this second sister face, that came   20
Absolute, perfect, fair without a flaw,
    Again the same?

III
VENICE

Out of the dark pure twilight, where the stream
Flows glimmering, streaked by many a birdlike bark
That skims the gloom whence towers and bridges gleam
    Out of the dark.

Once more a face no glance might choose but mark
Shone pale and bright, with eyes whose deep slow beam
Made quick the twilight, lifeless else and stark.

The same it seemed, or mystery made it seem,   30
As those before beholden; but St Mark

Ruled here the ways that showed it like a dream
   Out of the dark.

On an Old Roundel

Translated by D. G. Rossetti from the French of Villon

I

Death, from thy rigour a voice appealed,
And men still hear what the sweet cry saith,
Crying aloud in thine ears fast sealed,
     Death.

As a voice in a vision that vanisheth,
Through the grave's gate barred and the portal steeled
The sound of the wail of it travelleth.

Wailing aloud from a heart unhealed,
It woke response of melodious breath
From lips now too by thy kiss congealed,
     Death.

II

Ages ago, from the lips of a sad glad poet
Whose soul was a wild dove lost in the whirling snow,
The soft keen plaint of his pain took voice to show it
     Ages ago.

So clear, so deep, the divine drear accents flow,
No soul that listens may choose but thrill to know it,
Pierced and wrung by the passionate music's throe.

For us there murmurs a nearer voice below it,
Known once of ears that never again shall know,
Now mute as the mouth which felt death's wave o'erflow it
     Ages ago.

A Flower-Piece by Fantin

Heart's ease or pansy, pleasure or thought,
Which would the picture give us of these?
Surely the heart that conceived it sought
        Heart's ease.

Surely by glad and divine degrees
The heart impelling the hand that wrought
Wrought comfort here for a soul's disease.

Deep flowers, with lustre and darkness fraught,
From glass that gleams as the chill still seas
Lean and lend for a heart distraught
        Heart's ease.

A Sea-Mark

Rains have left the sea-banks ill to climb:
Waveward sinks the loosening seaboard's floor:
Half the sliding cliffs are mire and slime.
Earth, a fruit rain-rotted to the core,
Drops dissolving down in flakes, that pour
Dense as gouts from eaves grown foul with grime.
One sole rock which years that scathe not score
Stands a sea-mark in the tides of time.

Time were even as even the rainiest clime,
Life were even as even this lapsing shore,   10
Might not aught outlive their trustless prime:
Vainly fear would wail or hope implore,
Vainly grief revile or love adore
Seasons clothed in sunshine, rain, or rime.

Now for me one comfort held in store
Stands a sea-mark in the tides of time.

Once, by fate's default or chance's crime,
Each apart, our burdens each we bore;
Heard, in monotones like bells that chime,
Chime the sounds of sorrows, float and soar   20
Joy's full carols, near or far before;
Heard not yet across the alternate rhyme
Time's tongue tell what sign set fast of yore
Stands a sea-mark in the tides of time.

Friend, the sign we knew not heretofore
Towers in sight here present and sublime.
Faith in faith established evermore
Stands a sea-mark in the tides of time.

To a Seamew

When I had wings, my brother,
    Such wings were mine as thine:
Such life my heart remembers
In all as wild Septembers
As this when life seems other,
    Though sweet, than once was mine;
When I had wings, my brother,
    Such wings were mine as thine.

Such life as thrills and quickens
    The silence of thy flight,   10
Or fills thy note's elation
With lordlier exultation
Than man's, whose faint heart sickens
    With hopes and fears that blight
Such life as thrills and quickens
    The silence of thy flight.

Thy cry from windward clanging
   Makes all the cliffs rejoice;
Though storm clothe seas with sorrow,
Thy call salutes the morrow;   20
While shades of pain seem hanging
   Round earth's most rapturous voice,
Thy cry from windward clanging
   Makes all the cliffs rejoice.

We, sons and sires of seamen,
   Whose home is all the sea,
What place man may, we claim it;
But thine – whose thought may name it?
Free birds live higher than freemen,
   And gladlier ye than we –   30
We, sons and sires of seamen,
   Whose home is all the sea.

For you the storm sounds only
   More notes of more delight
Than earth's in sunniest weather:
When heaven and sea together
Join strengths against the lonely
   Lost bark borne down by night,
For you the storm sounds only
   More notes of more delight.   40

With wider wing, and louder
   Long clarion-call of joy,
Thy tribe salutes the terror
Of darkness, wild as error,
But sure as truth, and prouder
   Than waves with man for toy;
With wider wing, and louder
   Long clarion-call of joy.

The wave's wing spreads and flutters,
   The wave's heart swells and breaks;   50
One moment's passion thrills it,

One pulse of power fulfils it
And ends the pride it utters
  When, loud with life that quakes,
The wave's wing spreads and flutters,
  The wave's heart swells and breaks.

But thine and thou, my brother,
  Keep heart and wing more high
Than aught may scare or sunder;
The waves whose throats are thunder   60
Fall hurtling each on other,
  And triumph as they die;
But thine and thou, my brother,
  Keep heart and wing more high.

More high than wrath or anguish,
  More strong than pride or fear,
The sense or soul half hidden
In thee, for us forbidden,
Bids thee nor change nor languish,
  But live thy life as here,   70
More high than wrath or anguish,
  More strong than pride or fear.

We are fallen, even we, whose passion
  On earth is nearest thine;
Who sing, and cease from flying;
Who live, and dream of dying:
Grey time, in time's grey fashion,
  Bids wingless creatures pine:
We are fallen, even we, whose passion
  On earth is nearest thine.   80

The lark knows no such rapture,
  Such joy no nightingale,
As sways the songless measure
Wherein thy wings take pleasure:
Thy love may no man capture,
  Thy pride may no man quail;

The lark knows no such rapture,
　　Such joy no nightingale.

And we, whom dreams embolden,
　　We can but creep and sing　　　　　　　90
And watch through heaven's waste hollow
The flight no sight may follow
To the utter bourne beholden
　　Of none that lack thy wing:
And we, whom dreams embolden,
　　We can but creep and sing.

Our dreams have wings that falter,
　　Our hearts bear hopes that die;
For thee no dream could better
A life no fears may fetter,　　　　　　　100
A pride no care can alter,
　　That wots not whence or why
Our dreams have wings that falter,
　　Our hearts bear hopes that die.

With joy more fierce and sweeter
　　Than joys we deem divine
Their lives, by time untarnished,
Are girt about and garnished,
Who match the wave's full metre
　　And drink the wind's wild wine　　　110
With joy more fierce and sweeter
　　Than joys we deem divine.

Ah, well were I for ever,
　　Wouldst thou change lives with me,
And take my song's wild honey,
And give me back thy sunny
Wide eyes that weary never,
　　And wings that search the sea;
Ah, well were I for ever,
　　Wouldst thou change lives with me.　　120

Beachy Head: September 1886

The Lake of Gaube

The sun is lord and god, sublime, serene,
    And sovereign on the mountains: earth and air
Lie prone in passion, blind with bliss unseen
    By force of sight and might of rapture, fair
      As dreams that die and know not what they were.
The lawns, the gorges, and the peaks, are one
Glad glory, thrilled with sense of unison
In strong compulsive silence of the sun.

Flowers dense and keen as midnight stars aflame
And living things of light like flames in flower   10
That glance and flash as though no hand might tame
    Lightnings whose life outshone their stormlit hour
      And played and laughed on earth, with all their power
Gone, and with all their joy of life made long
And harmless as the lightning life of song,
Shine sweet like stars when darkness feels them strong.

The deep mild purple flaked with moonbright gold
    That makes the scales seem flowers of hardened light,
The flamelike tongue, the feet that noon leaves cold,
    The kindly trust in man, when once the sight   20
      Grew less than strange, and faith bade fear take flight,
Outlive the little harmless life that shone
And gladdened eyes that loved it, and was gone
Ere love might fear that fear had looked thereon.

Fear held the bright thing hateful, even as fear,
    Whose name is one with hate and horror, saith
That heaven, the dark deep heaven of water near,
    Is deadly deep as hell and dark as death.
      The rapturous plunge that quickens blood and breath
With pause more sweet than passion, ere they strive   30
To raise again the limbs that yet would dive
Deeper, should there have slain the soul alive.

As the bright salamander in fire of the noonshine exults and is
    glad of his day,

The spirit that quickens my body rejoices to pass from the
    sunlight away,
To pass from the glow of the mountainous flowerage, the high
    multitudinous bloom,
Far down through the fathomless night of the water, the gladness
    of silence and gloom.
Death-dark and delicious as death in the dream of a lover and
    dreamer may be,
It clasps and encompasses body and soul with delight to be living
    and free:
Free utterly now, though the freedom endure but the space of a
    perilous breath,
And living, though girdled about with the darkness and coldness
    and strangeness of death: 40
Each limb and each pulse of the body rejoicing, each nerve of the
    spirit at rest,
All sense of the soul's life rapture, a passionate peace in its
    blindness blest.
So plunges the downward swimmer, embraced of the water
    unfathomed of man,
The darkness unplummeted, icier than seas in mid-winter, for
    blessing or ban;
And swiftly and sweetly, when strength and breath fall short, and
    the dive is done,
Shoots up as a shaft from the dark depth shot, sped straight into
    sight of the sun;
And sheer through the snow-soft water, more dark than the roof
    of the pines above,
Strikes forth, and is glad as a bird whose flight is impelled and
    sustained of love.
As a sea-mew's love of the sea-wind breasted and ridden for
    rapture's sake
Is the love of his body and soul for the darkling delight of the
    soundless lake: 50
As the silent speed of a dream too living to live for a thought's
    space more
Is the flight of his limbs through the still strong chill of the
    darkness from shore to shore.
Might life be as this is and death be as life that casts off time as a
    robe,

The likeness of infinite heaven were a symbol revealed of the lake
    of Gaube.

Whose thought has fathomed and measured
    The darkness of life and of death,
The secret within them treasured,
    The spirit that is not breath?
Whose vision has yet beholden
    The splendour of death and of life?
Though sunset as dawn be golden,   60
    Is the word of them peace, not strife?
Deep silence answers: the glory
    We dream of may be but a dream,
And the sun of the soul wax hoary
    As ashes that show not a gleam.
But well shall it be with us ever
    Who drive through the darkness here,
If the soul that we live by never,
    For aught that a lie saith, fear.   70

In a Rosary

Through the low grey archway children's feet that pass
Quicken, glad to find the sweetest haunt of all.
Brightest wildflowers gleaming deep in lustiest grass,
Glorious weeds that glisten through the green sea's glass,
Match not now this marvel, born to fade and fall.

Roses like a rainbow wrought of roses rise
Right and left and forward, shining toward the sun.
Nay, the rainbow lit of sunshine droops and dies
Ere we dream it hallows earth and seas and skies;
Ere delight may dream it lives, its life is done.   10

Round the border hemmed with high deep hedges round
Go the children, peering over or between

Where the dense bright oval wall of box inwound,
Reared about the roses fast within it bound,
Gives them grace to glance at glories else unseen.

Flower outlightening flower and tree outflowering tree
Feed and fill the sense and spirit full with joy.
Nought awhile they know of outer earth and sea:
Here enough of joy it is to breathe and be:
Here the sense of life is one for girl and boy.   20

Heaven above them, bright as children's eyes or dreams,
Earth about them, sweet as glad soft sleep can show
Earth and sky and sea, a world that scarcely seems
Even in children's eyes less fair than life that gleams
Through the sleep that none but sinless eyes may know.

Near beneath, and near above, the terraced ways
Wind or stretch and bask or blink against the sun.
Hidden here from sight on soft or stormy days
Lies and laughs with love toward heaven, at silent gaze,
All the radiant rosary – all its flowers made one.   30

All the multitude of roses towering round
Dawn and noon and night behold as one full flower,
Fain of heaven and loved of heaven, curbed and crowned,
Raised and reared to make this plot of earthly ground
Heavenly, could but heaven endure on earth an hour.

Swept away, made nothing now for ever, dead,
Still the rosary lives and shines on memory, free
Now from fear of death or change as childhood, fled
Years on years before its last live leaves were shed:
None may mar it now, as none may stain the sea.   40

Notes

p. 3 *The Nightingale*: **32** the Greek poet Sappho of Lesbos (*c.* 600 BC). Legend tells how she committed suicide for love by leaping into the sea from the Leucadian cliff. **45 as of early crimes:** in classical myth these crimes would be the rape and muting of Philomela by Tereus and the subsequent revengeful murder of Tereus's son Itylus by Philomela and Procne. See also 'Itylus', and Ovid, *Metamorphoses* VI, 424–674.

p. 4 *A Ballad of Life* and *A Ballad of Death*: These 'ballads' are imitations of Italian *canzoni* of the kind produced by Dante and Calvalcanti and translated by D. G. Rossetti in *The Early Italian Poets* (1861). **76 Borgia:** Lucretia Borgia (1480–1519), daughter of the notorious Rodrigo Borgia (1431–1503) who later became Pope Alexander VI. The Lucretia of common legend, famed for her beauty, charm and immorality, was one of Swinburne's heroines and featured in his unfinished prose romance *The Chronicle of Tebaldeo Tebaldei* (*c.* 1860–63). These ballads, related in style and content to this work, probably date to 1862–3. In 1876 Swinburne proposed to his publisher that in a new edition of *Poems and Ballads I* the epigraph 'In honorem D. Lucretiae Estensis Borgiae' ('In honour of Lady Lucretia Estense Borgia') be added to 'A Ballad of Life', and the epigraph 'In obitum D. Lucretiae Estensis Borgiae' ('On the death of Lady Lucretia Estense Borgia') be added to 'A Ballad of Death'. 'D' might also signify 'Divae' (Goddess).

p. 10 *The Triumph of Time*: Those interested in providing a biographical source for this poem and Swinburne's 'lost love' have long debated the identity of its female addressee. The most likely contender is generally now acknowledged as Swinburne's maternal cousin, Mary Gordon, who became engaged to Colonel Disney Leith towards the end of 1864. **170 The gate is strait:** Matt 7:14: 'Because strait *is* the gate . . .' **239 'What should such fellows as I do?':** *Hamlet* III.i.126–7. **323 There lived a singer:** the twelfth-century Provençal troubadour Jaufré Rudel who, hearing of the fame of the Princess of Tripoli, fell in love with her. While voyaging to see her, he became ill and seemingly died. When his ship docked, his body was taken to an inn and the Princess came to honour his body. As she took him in her arms, he revived briefly, thanked God for allowing him to see her, and then died in her embrace. **324 the tideless dolorous midland sea:** the Mediterranean, which Swinburne thought tame and dull.

p. 21 *Les Noyades*: The title refers to collective executions by drowning as authorised by the French revolutionary, Jean Baptiste Carrier, in 1793. Thomas Carlyle in *The French Revolution* (1837) describes the Noyades: 'women and men are tied together, feet and feet, hand and hands; and flung in: this they call *Marriage Républicain*, Republican Marriage'.

p. 23 *Itylus*: See also 'The Nightingale', p. 3. Swinburne follows the later Latin version of the nightingale myth, derived from Ovid's *Metamorphoses*, in which Philomela is transformed into a nightingale and her sister Procne a swallow. In this poem, the nightingale reproaches the swallow for forgetting their vengeful murder of Itylus, son of Procne and Tereus. **48 the feast of Daulis:** Daulis is a city in Phocis, a central country of Ancient Greece, where Philomela and Procne feed the unwitting Tereus with the flesh of his son. Hence the nightingale is often known as the 'Daulian bird'. **52 The woven web that was plain to follow:** the tapestry pictures by which the muted Philomela informs Procne of the crimes committed against her by Tereus.

p. 25 *Anactoria*: Anactoria, one of Sappho's loves, is celebrated by her in Fragment 16 *Poetarum Lesbiorum Fragmenta*, eds Edgar Lobel and Denys Page (Oxford: Clarendon Press, 1955). Sappho's most famous poem, now usually known as 'To a Beloved Girl', was traditionally called the 'Ode to Anactoria'. Swinburne incorporates phrases from this fragment and others by Sappho into 'Anactoria', but the poem is very much his own.

The prefatory epigraph means, 'Whose love would you entreat, having vainly ensnared her?' and is Swinburne's deft reconstruction of the fragmentary Greek text of Sappho's 'Ode to Aphrodite' (Fragment 1, Lobel and Page) at the point where Aphrodite is imagined as speaking to Sappho. The text is more usually reconstructed so that it translates, 'Whom shall I persuade this time to take you back, yet once again, to her love?' **22 Erotion or Erinna:** a male or a female lover, although the name 'Erotion', which means 'little Eros (or Cupid)' or 'dedicated to Eros' is neuter in Greek. 'Erotion' is also title of another poem by Swinburne that was written to accompany a painting by his friend Simeon Solomon

(1840–1905). Erinna was one of Sappho's loves and is also the subject of another painting by Solomon 'Sappho and Erinna' (1864). **64 Paphos:** ancient city on the west coast of Cyprus at the spot where Aphrodite was born from the sea and the site of her most famous shrine. **73–4 'Who doth thee wrong, Sappho?':** quoted from Sappho's 'Ode to Aphrodite'. **169 Pleiads:** seven daughters of Atlas who were chased by Orion until the gods took pity on them and turned them into a constellation. Sappho mentions them in one of the fragments assigned to her authorship in the nineteenth century. **195 The high Pierian flower:** Pieria, in Macedonia, is the birthplace of the Muses. Sappho's Fragment 55 (Lobel and Page), which Swinburne follows here, speaks of 'roses of Pieria' as a sign of artistic fame. **286 Atthis:** one of Sappho's former female loves, mentioned in Fragment 49 (Lobel and Page). **302 Lotus and Lethe:** symbols of forgetfulness. The lotus fruit, like the waters of the underworld river of Lethe, had the power to make those who partook of it forget their past lives. **304 insuperable sea:** Sappho concludes this poem by meditating her suicidal leap into the sea.

p. 33 _Hermaphroditus_: The concluding epigraphic reference (p. 35) translates as 'At the Louvre Museum, March 1863' and thus directs the reader to the famous antique statue of an hermaphrodite held by the museum which had attracted the attention of various nineteenth-century French writers read by Swinburne. Among these was Théophile Gautier, who celebrated the statue in his poem 'Contralto' (1849) and his novel _Mademoiselle de Maupin_ (1835). In his response to his reviewers, _Notes on Poems and Reviews_ (London: Savill and Edwards, 1866), Swinburne also refers to Shelley's description of the hermaphrodite in 'The Witch of Atlas' (1824). The story of Hermaphroditus, a boy who is turned into a dual-sexed being, is told by Ovid in his _Metamorphoses_ IV, 285–388. Salmacis, a nymph, attempts to seduce the boy when he bathes in her pool. As they struggle in the water, the gods heed her prayers, and boy and nymph are united in the form of an hermaphrodite. (There is a good scholarly edition of _Notes on Poems and Reviews_ in _Swinburne Replies: Notes on Poems and Reviews, Under the Microscope, and Dedicatory Epistle_, ed. Clyde Kenneth Hyder (Syracuse, New York: Syracuse University Press, 1966).

p. 35 _Fragoletta_: Fragoletta (Italian for 'Little strawberry') is the name of an 1829 novel by Henri de Latouche whose eponymous heroine realises her ambiguous sexuality when she encounters an hermaphrodite statue in the gallery of Naples. 'Love', apostrophised in the first stanza, is Cupid or Eros, son of Venus-Aphrodite, and is traditionally represented as blind. See also the last line of 'Hermaphroditus', p. 35.

p. 37 *Anima Anceps*: The Latin title translates as 'the wavering or undecided mind'.

p. 39 *In the Orchard*: The poem's subtitle 'Provençal Burden' ('burden' meaning 'refrain') indicates that Swinburne is imitating the medieval poetry of Southern France and in particular the *alba*, or dawn poem, which deals with the theme of lovers parting at sunrise. There is a similarity between this poem and one of the most famous Provençal *albas* whose refrain 'Oy Dieus, oy Dieus, de l'alba! tan tost ve' translates as 'Oh God! Oh God! The dawn how soon it comes!'

p. 40 *The Leper*: The epigraph in late medieval French which accompanies this poem was invented by Swinburne. It translates as: 'At that time there were in that country numerous lepers and people similarly afflicted which greatly displeased the king, since God must have been grievously angered. Then it came about that a well-born young woman called Yolande de Sallières was struck down and completely wasted by this loathsome evil; her friends and relatives, seeing only the fear of God, banished her from their houses, and never again wished to receive or to comfort a thing cursed by God, stinking and abominable to all people. This lady had been extremely beautiful and gracefully formed; she made her body freely available and led a lascivious life. However, none of the lovers who had so many times and so tenderly embraced and kissed her wanted any more to give hospitality to such an ugly woman and so hateful a sinner. One single clerk, who was formerly her serving-man and go-between in love-affairs, took her in and concealed her in a small hut. There the wicked young thing died an evil death in great unhappiness. And after her died that same clerk who, through great love, had for six months cared for her, washed, dressed, and undressed her every day with his own hands. It was even said that this wicked man and cursed clerk, recalling the former great beauty of this woman, now wasted, took pleasure in kissing her many times on her filthy and leprous mouth, and in circling her softly with his loving hands. And he died of that same hateful disease. This happened near Fontainebellant en Gastinois. And when King Philip heard of this occurrence he wondered at it greatly.' (Translation by Julia Boffey.) **11 clerk:** man in a religious order, cleric, clergyman. In the Middle Ages when writing skills were limited to the clergy, the office of scribe would be undertaken by a cleric.

p. 45 Rondel: The terms 'rondeau' and 'rondel' are used for a variety of short fixed French poetic forms and, in the fifteenth century, were used interchangeably. The conventional rondeau consists of thirteen lines, having only two rhymes throughout, and with the opening words used twice as a refrain. It is a poetic form much used and adapted by Swinburne. This early rondel has twelve lines and five rhymes.

p. 46 Before the Mirror: written to accompany the picture 'The Little White Girl' (1864) by James Abbott McNeill Whistler (1834–1903).

p. 48 The Garden of Proserpine: Proserpine is goddess of the Underworld, and here of sleep and death. Her emblematic flower is the poppy, associated with sleep for its opiate properties.

p. 51 The Sundew: an insectivorous marsh plant native to the Isle of Wight and the Borders. Insects are caught on the sticky droplets which sparkle on its leaves. The sundew's combination of vegetable and animal qualities make it a characteristically Swinburnean plant.

p. 52 Sapphics: written in Sapphics (i.e., using the characteristic metrical stanza of Sappho). This is a particularly difficult prosodic form to use well in English and Swinburne is one of the few poets who succeeds with it. The poem again draws on Sappho's 'Ode to Aphrodite' with its vision of the goddess of love, but in Swinburne's poem Aphrodite is the goddess of heterosexual love who is rejected by Sappho. **16 Mitylene**: birthplace of Sappho on Lesbos. **30 the tenth, the Lesbian**: Sappho was commonly honoured as 'the tenth Muse'. **75 Ghosts of outcast women**: allusion to the two lesbian poems by Baudelaire entitled *Femmes Damnées*.

p. 55 August: This early poem, published in *The Spectator*, 6 September 1862, when it accompanied Swinburne's essay on Baudelaire, was admired by the French poet. The poem is slightly reminiscent of Baudelaire's famous synaesthetic sonnet 'Correspondances'.

p. 57 Hertha: On 20 February 1875 Swinburne wrote, 'of all I have done I rate Hertha highest as a single piece'. Hertha is the Teutonic earth goddess, represented in this poem as the source of all things. **18 before God was, I**

am: cf. John 8:58. **76 tripod:** three-legged vessel used as a seat by the oracular priestess of Apollo at Delphi, and thereby representative of priesthood. **115 The tree many-rooted:** Swinburne alludes to *Yggdrasil*, the world tree of Norse myth whose roots and branches connect heaven, earth and hell.

p. 66 *Cor Cordium*: Commemorates the poet Percy Bysshe Shelley (1792–1822) on whose tombstone in Rome the words 'Cor Cordium' ('Heart of Hearts') are inscribed.

p. 69 *Relics*: White laurustine is an evergreen flowering shrub. The flower conjures up past memories of the West Undercliff, near East Dene on the Isle of Wight and the town of San Gimignano, Italy, with its thirteen towers and its church of Santa Fina.

p. 75 *On the Cliffs*: The epigraph 'sweet-voiced nightingale' is a translation of Sappho, Fragment 136 (Lobel and Page). Swinburne addresses the nightingale as a composite identity comprised of woman (Sappho), god (Apollo, god of the sun, of prophecy and poetry) and bird. **49–55 strange children ... sinless matricide:** The Furies, daughters of Nox (Night), protested in vain against the murder of Clytemnestra by her son Orestes; he was acquitted by Athene who ruled the killing licit revenge for Clytemnestra's murder of Agamemnon. See Aeschylus' play *Eumenides*. **115 Rathe:** early. **141 *Ah, ah, the doom*:** Swinburne quotes the reply of the prophetess Cassandra in Aeschylus' *Agamemnon* (1146–9) who is compared by the Chorus to the sorrowful nightingale. Taken from Troy by Agamemnon as his bondslave and mistress, Cassandra foresees that she and Agamemnon will be killed by Clytemnestra in Argos and wishes for the better fate of the nightingale. **152 entangling dragnet:** used not only in a metaphorical sense, for Clytemnestra snares Agamemnon in a net before she and her lover, Aegisthus, kill him. Clytemnestra then murders Cassandra. **157 Who thought with craft:** Cassandra persuaded Apollo, god of prophecy, to give her the gift of foresight in return for her love, but having achieved her desire she refused to honour her part in the bargain, and was punished by him to the end that no one would believe her prophecies. **163 That strange-eyed spirit-wounded strange-tongued slave:** Cassandra, the bondslave of Agamemnon, has foresight. Clytemnestra speculates whether she speaks 'an unintelligible barbarian tongue' (*Agamemnon*, 1051). **164 houndlike:** Cassandra is compared by the Chorus to a hound scenting blood (*Agamemnon*, 1093–4). She hesitates to enter Agamemnon's palace because she says the house smells of blood (*Agamemnon*, 1309). **167 hers**: Aphrodite's. Even Aphrodite, goddess of heterosexual love, gives Sappho, an adherent of lesbian love, a 'guerdon' or reward for her song. **171 pale princess-priest**: Cassandra is daughter of King Priam of Troy. **176 him that only gives**: Apollo. **229–30 by thine only name, Sappho**: Swinburne refers to his 'true' identification of the nightingale with Sappho which he says in a letter to Watts-Dunton (30 July 1879) he discovered when a schoolboy. **237 ere sooth was seen**: before I saw the truth. **245 Majano**: Swinburne recollects how visiting Maiano in Italy in 1864, he recited his poems to the local nightingales. **299 *O thou of divers-coloured mind***: a translation of the opening of the 'Ode to Aphrodite'. **320 No swan-song**: Sappho's fiery last song is seen as triumphant and defiant rather than tragic and pathetic. **325 *I loved thee ... Atthis***: Sappho, Fragment 49 (Lobel and Page). **333 *Child of God***: another rendering of the opening of the 'Ode to Aphrodite'. **417 small dark body's Lesbian loveliness**: An ancient commentator, the scholiast on Lucian's portraits, compared Sappho to the nightingale because she was small and dark. Swinburne transforms this originally unflattering remark into praise. **422 sevenfold shields**: made of seven reinforcing layers, like Ajax's shield in the *Iliad* VII, 222–3, which is made of seven ox-hides.

p. 87 *The Queen's Pleasance*: The extract is taken from the second canto of Swinburne's epic poem *Tristram of Lyonesse* which describes the developing relationship between Tristram and Iseult, who fall in love when they drink a love-potion on their sea-voyage to Tintagel where Iseult is to become wife of King Mark. The marriage takes place but the pair become lovers. When Mark is forced to give Iseult to the knight Palamon as the result of an unlucky pledge, Tristram fights with Palamon and rescues Iseult. The couple then take to the woods where they live and love undisturbed for an idyllic three months.

p. 89 *The Lute and the Lyre*: Formerly a synonym for the rondeau or rondel, the 'roundel' is now usually associated with the variant form introduced by Swinburne. The conventional thirteen-line French rondeau consists of three stanzas rhyming aabba aab aabba with only two rhymes used throughout. The first word or phrase becomes a refrain which is repeated in lines eight and thirteen. In *A Century of Roundels*, Swinburne developed his characteristic roundel form which comprises eleven lines and three stanzas, with the refrain repeated in lines four and eleven.

p. 89 *Plus Intra*: translates as 'More within'. 'Soul within sense' is a recurrent Swinburnean phrase.

p. 90 *Three Faces*: A letter to Watts-Dunton (24 January 1875), explains the inspiration for this poem: 'As to women, I saw at Venice one of the three most beautiful I ever saw (the other two were one at Genoa, the other at Ventimiglia in the Riviera.')

p. 92 *On an Old Roundel*: In this poem comprising two roundels, Swinburne alludes to Dante Gabriel Rossetti's translation of Villon's roundel 'To Death, of his Lady'. Swinburne implies the affinity between Villon and Rossetti, brought about by the death of Rossetti's wife Elizabeth Siddal in 1862. Moreover Rossetti's own recent death in 1882 – 'From lips now too by thy kiss congealed' – adds an extra note of pathos.

p. 93 *A Flower-Piece by Fantin*: Henri Fantin-Latour (1836–1904), a French painter noted in England for his fine still life and flower paintings. Swinburne was introduced to him by Whistler in 1863. The roundel puns on 'pansy' derived from the French common name for the flower, *pensée*, which also means 'thought'. 'Heartsease' is the old-fashioned English name for the pansy.

p. 94 *To a Seamew*: For Swinburne's identification of himself with the seamew (the common seagull), see also the conclusion to 'On the Cliffs', p. 75.

p. 98 *The Lake of Gaube*: Swinburne visited the Lake of Gaube in 1862 during a trip to the Pyrenees. He describes swimming in the lake and taming salamanders in an essay of 1890 on Victor Hugo's 'Notes of Travel'. Traditionally understood as a union of hot and cold, the salamander, or lizard, was imagined to live in fire without any harm to itself, and was often held to represent the fire of the alchemists. The goal of the alchemical opus, known as the Philosophers' Stone, is said to be 'salamandrine' in its final state of perfect indestructibility where it converts all imperfection with which it comes into contact into its own perfection.

p. 100 *In a Rosary*: Rosary is an archaic word for a rose garden, but in the alchemical lexicon it also represents an area of esoteric knowledge.

Acknowledgements

My acknowledgements to Julia Boffey, Mike Edwards and Ros Allen, my colleagues at Queen Mary and Westfield, for help and advice regarding translation.